# Benson Ebinne
(M.S., M.Div.)

# Meditations for a *Quiet Place*

## Devotional for Thoughtful and Biblical Living

Copyright @2021 by Benson Ebinne

All rights reserved. No part of this book may be reproduced in any form or by any electronic or mechanical means, including information storage and retrieval systems, without permission in writing from the publisher, except by reviewers, who may quote brief passages in a review.

This publication contains the opinions and ideas of its author. It is intended to provide helpful and informative material on the subjects addressed in the publication. The author and publisher specifically disclaim all responsibility for any liability, loss or risk, personal or otherwise, which is incurred as a consequence, directly or indirectly, of the use and application of any of the contents of this book.

WORKBOOK PRESS LLC
187 E Warm Springs Rd,
Suite B285, Las Vegas, NV 89119, USA

| | |
|---|---|
| Website: | https://workbookpress.com/ |
| Hotline: | 1-888-818-4856 |
| Email: | admin@workbookpress.com |

Ordering Information:
Quantity sales. Special discounts are available on quantity purchases by corporations, associations, and others.
For details, contact the publisher at the address above.

ISBN-13:   978-1-953839-73-2 (Paperback Version)
           978-1-953839-74-9 (Digital Version)

REV. DATE: 06/01/2021

# Contents

Teachable Learning . . . . . . . . . . . . . . . . . . . . . . . . . . . . . . 7
A Matter of Love . . . . . . . . . . . . . . . . . . . . . . . . . . . . . . . . 9
A Crown of Righteousness . . . . . . . . . . . . . . . . . . . . . . . . 11
A Sacred Shelter . . . . . . . . . . . . . . . . . . . . . . . . . . . . . . . . 13
Reverence . . . . . . . . . . . . . . . . . . . . . . . . . . . . . . . . . . . . . 15
Dynamite or Dynamo . . . . . . . . . . . . . . . . . . . . . . . . . . . 17
Hallelujah . . . . . . . . . . . . . . . . . . . . . . . . . . . . . . . . . . . . . 19
Majoring in Minors . . . . . . . . . . . . . . . . . . . . . . . . . . . . . 21
Who Is My Neighbor? . . . . . . . . . . . . . . . . . . . . . . . . . . . 23
What is Worship? . . . . . . . . . . . . . . . . . . . . . . . . . . . . . . 25
Meditation . . . . . . . . . . . . . . . . . . . . . . . . . . . . . . . . . . . . 27
Satisfaction . . . . . . . . . . . . . . . . . . . . . . . . . . . . . . . . . . . 29
Gratitude . . . . . . . . . . . . . . . . . . . . . . . . . . . . . . . . . . . . . 31
Prayer and Praise . . . . . . . . . . . . . . . . . . . . . . . . . . . . . . 33
Keeping the Faith . . . . . . . . . . . . . . . . . . . . . . . . . . . . . . 35
Openness and Closeness . . . . . . . . . . . . . . . . . . . . . . . . 37
Faith and Righteousness . . . . . . . . . . . . . . . . . . . . . . . . 39
Detestable Things . . . . . . . . . . . . . . . . . . . . . . . . . . . . . . 41
Blasphemy . . . . . . . . . . . . . . . . . . . . . . . . . . . . . . . . . . . . 43
Galilee of the Gentiles . . . . . . . . . . . . . . . . . . . . . . . . . . 45
Hygiene . . . . . . . . . . . . . . . . . . . . . . . . . . . . . . . . . . . . . . 47
Wisdom and Satisfaction . . . . . . . . . . . . . . . . . . . . . . . 49
Good Grief . . . . . . . . . . . . . . . . . . . . . . . . . . . . . . . . . . . 51
Prayer and Fasting . . . . . . . . . . . . . . . . . . . . . . . . . . . . . 53
Casting Your Bread on the Water . . . . . . . . . . . . . . . . 55
Like Master Like Servant . . . . . . . . . . . . . . . . . . . . . . . 57
The Original Voice . . . . . . . . . . . . . . . . . . . . . . . . . . . . . 59
Knowing the Will of God . . . . . . . . . . . . . . . . . . . . . . . 61
Conservative Love . . . . . . . . . . . . . . . . . . . . . . . . . . . . . 63

| | |
|---|---|
| Vigilance | 65 |
| Spiritual Stirring | 67 |
| Praying to Be Answered | 69 |
| So Near and So Far | 71 |
| Heart Conditioning | 73 |
| Clear Conscience | 75 |
| True and Reasonable | 77 |
| The Whole Truth | 79 |
| The Master and His Servant | 81 |
| The New Covenant | 83 |
| Honoring God | 85 |
| Dust in the Wind? | 87 |
| Prayer Principles | 89 |
| Shalom | 91 |
| Lord Have Mercy | 93 |
| The Hope of God's Glory | 95 |
| Fair Play | 97 |
| Covetousness | 99 |
| Fountain of Life | 101 |
| Dominion and Glory | 103 |
| A Note of Thanks | 105 |
| Selected Poems by Benson Ebinne | 106 |
| Notes | 114 |
| Acknowledgments | 115 |

# *Teachable Learning*

*Teach me, O LORD, to follow your decrees; then I will keep them to the end.*

*Psalm 119:33*

Willingness to learn is an important component in the process of teaching. The language of the Old Testament in its original form is Hebrew. In this language learning and teaching are verbs with the same word. It goes without saying that learning and teaching go together. Correct teaching begets proper learning (at least, in theory). As far as the scriptures are concerned the teacher is the Lord. The psalmist prayed to be taught by the divine teacher.

The psalmist's desire for efficacious learning is evident in the expressed need to obey with all his heart (v.34). There is an obedience training school in St. Louis, Missouri. It goes by the name "Sit Means Sit." The dog trainer commonly known as The Dog Whisperer can take a rambunctious dog and turn it into a calm, obedient, and compliant animal in just a few minutes. In its new state the dog remains undisturbed by the very things that used to trigger undesirable behavior. While dogs can obey without questions, for humans, commands or laws may be subject to personal interpretation or even misrepresentation. A student with an attitude that is conducive to learning can be a fertile ground for a teacher. Therefore, the removal of impediments is important. "Direct me ... Turn my heart ... Turn my eyes ... not toward selfish gain ... Turn my eyes away from worthless things ..." (119:35-37).

Because learning is a means to an end, people are taught or trained so that they would do what is right. The scriptures are the source of teachings for righteousness. "How can a young man keep his way pure? By living according to your word" (119:9). In the New Testament this is made clear by Paul's exhortation to Timothy his understudy and convert. "... from infancy you have known the holy Scriptures, which are able to make you wise for salvation through faith in Christ Jesus.

All Scripture is God-breathed and is suitable for teaching, rebuking, correcting and training in righteousness, so that the man of God may be thoroughly equipped for every good work" (2 Timothy 3:15-16). All believers, like the psalmist, will do well to desire the Lord as their teacher, because He is the perfect teacher. He is the one who can circumcise their spiritual hearts to take away the kind of stubbornness or stiff neck, that impedes learning (Deuteronomy 10:16).

Suggested Text: Psalm 119:33-40.
Suggested Prayer: Teach me to do your will, for you are my God … for I am your servant" (Psalm 143:10-12).

Benson Ebinne

# *A Matter of Love*

*Teacher, which is the greatest commandment in the Law?*

*Matthew 22:36*

 The Pharisees were a Jewish sect known for their expertise in the Law (the Torah, or the first five books of the Bible). One such expert was delegated to test Jesus, in an attempt to challenge his authority. Previously, the Herodians and Sadducees had taken their respective turns to test Jesus concerning payments of taxes, and the resurrection (Matthew 22:23-33). Jesus' response to the Pharisee was taken both from Deuteronomy 6:5, and Leviticus 19:18, respectively. Essentially, the greatest command is to love the LORD without reservation. This, the greatest commandment, has a follow-up, which is to love the neighbor unselfishly. "All the Law and the Prophets hang on these two commandments." The narrative does not give the Pharisee's reaction to this response. Laws are sometimes subject to interpretations (and sometimes misinterpretations). What does it mean to love an invisible being like the Lord, God of Israel, and do so with no reservation? What does it mean to love one's neighbor as oneself?

 Fidelity, allegiance, and devotion, together describe unadulterated love. In the context of worship, the Lord demands the people of God to be different from the pagans and their man-made gods. The God of Israel describes Himself as jealous. "You shall not bow down to them or worship them; for I, the LORD your God, am a jealous God" (Exodus 20:5). When people take the respect and honor due Him, and give it to idols, He becomes jealous. This is good jealousy, like a man's reaction when he finds another man flirting with his wife. A teacher might feel that way too, when he or she finds the students doing other things when they should be paying attention. To love the LORD with all of the heart, soul and mind, would require giving these three components of one's person unreservedly, in allegiance to God. The hymn writer, Frances Ridley Havergal, put it this way: "Take my life, and let it be / Consecrated, Lord to Thee. / Take my moments and my days; / Let them flow in ceaseless praise" (The Church Hymnary, Oxford University Press). Similarly, the psalmist wrote: "Give me understanding, and I will keep your law and obey it with all my heart" (Psalm 119:34). This understanding is an outgrowth of the gift of wisdom.

The Apostle James gave this exhortation in his epistle: "Who is wise and understanding among you? Let him show it by his good life, by deeds done in the humility that comes from wisdom… But the wisdom that comes from heaven is first of all pure; then peace loving, considerate, submissive, full of mercy and good fruit, impartial and sincere" (James 3:13, 17). Because the natural man cannot love God, let alone his fellow human unreservedly, he must get wisdom from above. Spiritual things are discerned by spiritually transformed lives (John 3:6-8). Love for God is related to love for the neighbor in that the ability flows from above to enable a horizontal effect. This love is pure, peace loving, considerate, submissive, full of mercy and good fruit, impartial and sincere (as stated by the Apostle James). But who is my neighbor? The answer comes by way of the Parable of the Good Samaritan given in Luke 10:25-37. Essentially, a neighbor is a person who needs the help that is in my power to provide unselfishly, like the Good Samaritan did for the helpless victim of robbery.

I have heard a preacher say that each individual in his or her interpersonal relationships is wishing either of these statements: "I love you" or "please love me." The most practical way to love an invisible God is to love one's brother or sister (1 John 4:11-21). To love the neighbor as yourself is to love sincerely (Romans 12:9). According to Jesus, wholehearted love for God, as well as sincere love for the neighbor, is the crux of the Law and the Prophets. The Ten Commandments, for instance, are a microcosm of love. The first four show us how to love God, while the last six show us how to love our fellow humans. The prophets were among other things, enforcers of the commandments, warning the covenant people whenever they strayed from its precepts, about the consequences. It is all a matter of love.

Suggested Text: 1 Corinthians 13.
Suggested Prayer: "Take my life and let it be consecrated Lord to thee."

*Benson Ebinne*

# *A Crown of Righteousness*

*Gray hair is a crown of splendor, it is attained by a righteous life.*

*Proverbs 16:31*

In most cases, gray hair is associated with advancing years. However, stress and other difficulties can cause a younger person to turn gray. In this text, gray hair will be in reference to old age. Church goers are likely familiar with the nursery rhyme: "Jesus loves the little children / All the children of the world / Red or yellow, black or white / They are precious in his sight, / Jesus loves the little children of the world." There may not be a similar song for the elderly, but they are equally precious to the Lord. In Leviticus 19:32 the Israelites were instructed to: "Rise in the presence of the aged, show respect for the elderly and revere your God. I am the LORD." God commands respect for the elderly. They are also precious in His sight.

So what? What has this to do with us in the modern era? The gray hair is compared to a crown of splendor. It is a glorious halo covering the head of an elder. There is something more. This status is not automatic. Merely growing gray hair is not a qualification for splendor or glory. "It is attained by a righteous life." Righteousness is equal to right standing with God. In the New Testament, Paul stated: "I have fought the good fight, I have finished the race, I have kept the faith. Now there is stored for me a crown of righteousness, which the Lord, the righteous Judge, will award to me on that day…" (2 Timothy 4:7-8). He was older at this stage than earlier when he encouraged Timothy to engage the pursuit of righteousness in his faith walk (1 Timothy 6:11). The Lord honors those who pursue righteousness. The Bible describes those who are plugged into this virtue, as "a tree planted by streams of water, which yields its fruit in season and whose leaf does not wither" (Psalm 1:3). Such people will prosper.

A person does not become righteous by doing righteous deeds. It is the other way around. Righteousness is a divine gift. The fear of the Lord is the beginning of wisdom (Proverbs 1:7, 9:10). "But the wisdom that comes from heaven is first of all pure; then peace loving, considerate, submissive, full of mercy and good fruit, impartial and sincere" (James 3:17). The tree in the reference above (Psalm 1:3), did not plant itself. Someone chose a suitable spot to do so. A God-fearing person has a heart that is planted by the river of living water. "The righteous will flourish like a palm tree, they will grow like the cedar of Lebanon; planted in the house of the LORD, they will flourish in the courts of our God. They will still bear fruit in old age, they will stay fresh and green" (Psalm 92:12-14).

Indeed, the individuals who have had a lifetime of fellowship with the Lord, meditating on His word, and walking in the paths of righteousness, cannot fail to have the crown of splendor as a present reality, and a crown of righteousness in the future of glory. We must rise in their presence and show them respect (Leviticus 19:32).

Suggested Text: Psalm 92.
Suggested Prayer: Psalm 8.

Benson Ebinne

# *A Sacred Shelter*

*I long to dwell in your tent forever
and take refuge in the shelter of your wings.*

*Psalm 61:4*

Although tent and tabernacle can be used interchangeably, it is not usual for believers to call their places of worship, tents. The preferred term is tabernacle. Faith Tabernacle, Brooklyn Tabernacle, to name a few, persist today because long ago, churches were named that way. Today, tents are associated more with camping, than places of worship.

For a nomad, a tent is a shelter; a refuge, from the elements as well as wild creatures. In ancient times, the Israelites, after leaving Egypt and on their way to freedom in the Promised Land, lived in tents. They also reserved a special tent to house the Ark of the Covenant, where Moses communed with the God of Israel (Exodus 33:7-11; Numbers 12:5, 10; Deuteronomy 31:14-15). This was a sanctuary: a sacred place, a focus of God's presence.

King David, centuries later, must have had this sacred place in mind when he wrote: "I long to dwell in your tent forever and take refuge in the shelter of your wings." His heart was overwhelmed (NKJV), or faint (NIV), or in despair (TEV). He might have been exhausted, depressed, or both. Wallowing in self-pity was not the solution. Climbing out of the pit of despair on to higher ground was a more viable option. Not just any ground, but a rock (v.2). He prayed for restoration: "Then I will sing praise to your name and fulfill my vows day after day" (v.8).

Many centuries later, Jesus of Nazareth instructed his disciples thus: "When you pray, go into your room, close the door and pray to your Father, who is unseen. Then your Father, who sees what is done in secret, will reward you" (Matthew 6:7). Your personal tent, tabernacle, or sanctuary, may be any special place you choose. In that personal place, mercy, grace, and restoration will be waiting and available to be received by faith. The Lord is a rewarder of those who seek Him earnestly (Hebrew 11:6). Those who draw near to Him, and seek help in their time of need, will find a shelter from the stormy blasts of life.

Suggested Text: Psalm 61

Suggested Prayer: "Surely goodness and mercy shall follow me all the days of my life; and I will dwell in the house of the LORD forever" (Psalm 23:6).

# *Reverence*

*The fear of the LORD is the beginning of wisdom,
and the knowledge of the Holy One is understanding.*

*Proverbs 9:10 (NKJV).*

What does it mean to fear the LORD? When I was a Sunday School teacher, I posed the same question to my class. Of the several answers I was given, one stood out. It came from a ten year old boy. He said: "it means I am afraid to do what God hates." When an individual is sensitive to the extent of avoiding what God forbids, such a person is on the side of wisdom. The word 'wise' in Hebrew, has a range of meanings including: "being skillful, shrewd, crafty, cunning, prudent, and ethical" (The Hebrew English Lexicon, by F. Brown, S. Driver, and C. Briggs, 2005). In the scriptures, wisdom is contrasted with scoffing (Proverbs 9:12), and foolishness (9:13). There are intelligent people who are not wise per se. Their wisdom is earthly, as exemplified by what high profile individuals say when they are caught in scandals. Their usual confessions include the fact that they had acted on account of poor judgment. "But if you have bitter envy and self-seeking in your hearts, do not boast and lie against the truth. This wisdom does not descend from above, but is earthly, sensual and demonic" (James 3:14-15, NKJV).

In Proverbs 9, wisdom and folly are personified picturing two female persons respectively. They send out invitations to the same group of people (9:4,16). The wise responders are interested in gaining understanding (v.6), and so they are on the path to life (v.11); whereas those who lack understanding and are conducive to seduction choose folly (v.17), and as such are doomed (v.18). The former group is oriented toward the fear (or reverence) of the LORD. The wisdom they get opens up a wealth of skills for Godly living. According to James in the New Testament, "the wisdom that is from above is first pure, then peaceable, gentle, willing to yield, full of mercy and good fruits, without partiality and without hypocrisy"

(James 3:17, NKJV).

I once read a cartoon depicting a straggler who came to a fork in his path. One direction was marked *Cheese and Crackers*, while the other was marked *The Meaning of Life*. We know that life is full of choices, some of which are more difficult than the others. Jesus said: "I am the way, the truth, and the life. No one comes to the Father except through Me" (John 14:6). He will give wisdom to those who seek to follow the path of righteousness because He is the wisdom of God.

Suggested Text: Proverbs 9.
Suggested Prayer: "So teach us to number our days that we may gain a heart of wisdom" (Psalm 90:12, NKJV).

Benson Ebinne

# *Dynamite or Dynamo*

*He who is slow to anger is better than the mighty, and he who rules his spirit than he who takes a city.*

*Proverbs 16:32, NKJV..*

Using his poetic method of contrasting parallels, King Solomon compares a patient and self-controlled man, with a warrior and conqueror. There are two forces at play in this picture and the end product is either destructive or constructive. An army commander in the act of taking a city is driven by anger and strength, both of which serve a purpose and the road to victory can be considered as destructive. On the other hand, there is the picture of a man who is "slow to anger" and also "controls his temper"; he is slow to heat up and he demonstrates a slow discharge of the heat. The outcome serves a constructive purpose as far as human interactions are concerned and this person can be regarded as a gentleman.

Why did King Solomon use this comparison? After all, does a warrior not serve a purpose? What about security and defense? As valuable as brute strength may be, there is something more powerful. In the scriptural scheme of things, constructive outcomes are better than destructive ones; and a self-controlled person is more powerful than a brave fighter. Because God has called believers to live righteously, they must exercise self-control. This virtue was epitomized in Jesus of Nazareth, during his earthly ministry. "When they hurled their insults at him, he did not retaliate; when he suffered he made no threats. Instead, he entrusted himself to him who judges justly" (1 Peter 2:23).

Does this mean that a believer in Christ should never be upset? No. There is a good way to be upset, and there is a bad way to be upset. Who then is the judge? It is the written word of God as found in the Bible. It illuminates and informs the believer's understanding and actions (Psalm 119:9, 130). Being upset and getting angry may go together in most cases, especially considering the provocation.

Two references from the New Testament present some insights into the subject of anger. "Everyone should be quick to listen, slow to speak and slow to become angry, for man's anger does not bring about the righteous life that God desires. Therefore ... humbly accept the word planted in you, which can save you" (James 1:20-21). Knowing and practicing God's word is how a person can begin to have self control. "In your anger do not sin. Do not let the sun go down while you are still angry" (Ephesians 4:26, an echo of Psalm 4:4). Like James, Paul does not rule out the possibility of becoming angry. James advocates a disciplined approach, to ensure that the reaction is in line with righteousness; whereas Paul cautions against falling into sin on account of it.

Dynamite and dynamos are power implements that produce different outcomes when they release power. The former is explosive with destructive capacity, and the latter generates electrical power in a controlled discharge. The believer who is indwelled by the Holy Spirit, is endowed with the potential for a controlled discharge of power to serve a constructive purpose. Self-control and gentleness are integral parts of the fruit of the Holy Spirit. As stated in Galatians 5:22, "the fruit of the Holy Spirit is love, joy, peace, patience, kindness, goodness, faithfulness, gentleness and self-control. Against such there is no law."

Suggested Text: Ephesians 4:17-32.

Suggested Prayer: "May the words of my mouth and the meditation of my heart be pleasing in your sight, O LORD, my Rock and my Redeemer" (Psalm 19:14).

# *Hallelujah*

*Come, bless the LORD, all you servants of the LORD, who stand by night in the house of the LORD.*

Psalm 134:1 (ESV).

The word bless is defined as: to make holy; to ask divine favor for; to endow (with); to make happy; to glorify; to make the sign of the Cross over (Webster's New World Dictionary). It is used three times in this psalm; imploring the LORD's servants, as well as invoking the LORD Himself.

What does it mean to bless the LORD? Is it to please or to glorify Him? Taking a cue from the translations that render the word as praise (NIV and TEV), we come closer to an answer. To praise someone is to say good, nice, or complimentary things to him or her. As a result, that person smiles and thanks you. The purpose of worship is to corporately express how worthy God is as the maker, and sustainer of everything. The word worship shares the same roots as the word *worth*. The LORD is worthy to be praised and is pleased to receive such adoration. "But the hour is coming and now is, when the true worshipers will worship the Father in spirit and truth; for the Father is seeking such to worship Him" (John 4:23, NKJV). Believers engage in this activity, through expressive prayers, singing, and standing in awe of their Maker.

In return, the LORD blesses His servants or worshipers. In the context of Psalm 134, thee servants are the Levite priests who stand in the holy place (sanctuary), day and night. The Master is obliged to care for and requite His servants. The LORD blesses His servants by endowing the servants or worshipers with grace and mercy. Grace is unmerited favor, while mercy is the withholding of merited disfavor. Mercy (translated from the Hebrew hesed) is a compound word meaning, steadfast love, or loving kindness.

Are you a servant of the LORD? Then praise Him in private, as well as in public worship. "Bless the LORD, all you servants of the LORD."

Suggested Text: Psalm 134.

Suggested Prayer: Glory be to You O Father. Sanctify me, that I may worship You in spirit and in truth, through Jesus Christ, who reigns with You in unity with the Holy Spirit. Amen.

*Benson Ebinne*

# *Majoring in Minors*

*You blind guides! You strain out a gnat but swallow a camel.*

*Matthew 23:24.*

While the first sentence above is clear and self-explanatory, the second one is not. It is possible to filter out a gnat as well as other impurities in water, to make it drinkable. Swallowing a camel on the other hand is a practical impossibility. A listener at the time of this utterance by Jesus, could readily understand his usage of a hyperbole ("An exaggerated statement often used as a figure of speech" - The American Heritage Dictionary). This statement came following the fourth of seven woes pronounced by Jesus against the Pharisees and the teachers of the law. These woes are listed in verses 13 to 29. Although the woes are not necessarily condemnations, they show Christ's indignation or anger against the Pharisees and the scribes for their notorious majoring in minors concerning the ritual laws and the moral laws of Moses. They failed to practice their teachings while making it difficult for their followers to practice the tedious legalisms that had been attached to the Mosaic laws. In the words of Jesus, "They tie up heavy loads and put them on men's shoulders, but they themselves are not willing to lift a finger to move them" (v.4). He surprisingly asked his audience to obey these teachers and do what they said, but not to "do what they do, for they do not practice what they preach" (v.3).

In our own modern times we know that there are similar situations of hypocrisy from leaders in the church. Should the people continue to listen to such leaders, or should they go somewhere else? First, let us look at a list of indictments against the Pharisees and the teachers of the law: blind guides - vv.16, 24; blind fools - v.17; blind men - vv.19, 26; whitewashed tombs - v.27; snakes and vipers - v.33. If we go by verse 3, we must obey their teachings while avoiding their practices. With a focus on verse 23, we can take a cue for differentiating between the majors and minors. The major issues of life center on "justice, mercy and faithfulness." There is an Old Testament equivalent of these three cardinal virtues in Micah 6:8 - "He has showed you, O man, what is good. And what does the LORD require of you? To act justly and to love mercy and to walk humbly before your God." Here, God sent the prophet Micah to remind the people about His faithfulness to them right from their deliverance from Egypt, and the passage through the wilderness, to the settlement in the Land of Promise. Yet, the people were preoccupied with rituals: "Will the LORD be pleased with thousands of rams, with ten thousand rivers of oil? Shall I offer my firstborn for my transgression, the fruit of my body for the sin of my soul?" (6:7). The answer to this self imposed dilemma is found in verse 8.

The LORD God is motivated by loving kindness in His dealings with mankind. When man is similarly motivated by love, he will see the importance of justice, mercy and faithfulness, in his interpersonal dealings. He will stop majoring in minors. He will avoid hypocrisy. He will love his neighbor as himself.

Suggested Text: Micah 6:1-8.
Suggested Prayer: Meditate on Hosea 6:8. Pray for grace to comprehend this principle.

Benson Ebinne

# *Who Is My Neighbor?*

*Love your neighbor as yourself.*

Matthew 22:39

I had a pastor who summarized all human needs for emotional well-being in two sentences: I love you. Please love me. According to him, each person you see is contemplating either one of these sentences. My first reaction was to deem it simplistic. With further reflection, it gradually made sense to me. Some time after that I saw a cartoon in a magazine depicting a small dog and a caged parrot in a nice home. The dog was looking at the parrot some six feet above it. The words attributed to it were a plaintiff, "Will it kill you if once in awhile you say, 'good dog'?"

The command to love the neighbor as oneself is recorded in Leviticus 19:18. The full text reads: "Do not seek revenge or bear a grudge against one of your people, but love your neighbor as yourself. I am the LORD." A few verses further down, a recommendation for the proper treatment of aliens or strangers, was given (vv.33-34). From this it can be inferred that the neighbor is not just the person living next door. Who is my neighbor? This very question was explicitly asked by a person who encountered Jesus, desiring to know what to do in order to inherit eternal life (Luke 10:25). Jesus referred him to Deuteronomy 6:5 and Leviticus 19:18 (two texts about loving God wholeheartedly, and loving the neighbor unselfishly). The man claimed to have kept both commands. But seeking to justify himself, he asked the question. The answer came from Jesus via the Parable of the Good Samaritan in Luke 10:30-37. This is the story of a victim of highway robbery who was wounded and left half dead. Two people, a priest and a Levite, passed him by but did nothing to help him. A third man, a businessman, had pity on him, gave him first aid, put him on his donkey, and took him to a wayside inn, to rest while he went to do his business. He promised to come back shortly and pay whatever bills were accumulated. When Jesus finished the story, he asked the enquirer who among the three men he thought was a neighbor to the victim. The obvious answer was the one who had pity on the victim. Then Jesus told him to go and do the same. In other words, his neighbor was any person that had a need for compassionate treatment.

How does this apply to Christians? The Apostle John taught that the person who claims to love God, should start by showing love to other people first (1 John 4:19-24). Paul wrote: "Love must be sincere" (Romans 12:9). James terms love for the neighbor, "the royal law" (James 2:8). Compassion is the virtue that moves one person to rise and help another person in need. Hospitals for instance, have been built and still stand today, because men and women of God were moved by compassion to help the sick with the love for God as the motivation. Good Samaritans are alive and well.

Suggested Text: 1 Corinthians 13.
Suggested Prayer: Lord, help me to be a Good Samaritan.

# *What is Worship?*

*For I know that the LORD is great,
and that our LORD is above all gods.
Whatsoever the LORD pleases He does, in heaven,
and in earth, in the seas, and all deep places.*

*Psalm 135:5-6, NKJV.*

Praise is reasoned adoration; a thankful acknowledgement of favors. Psalm 135 opens and closes with "Praise the LORD." Flattery is shallow praise. It can be insincere, and calculated to appeal to the vanity of the recipient. This is not what the psalmist is doing. He is aware of the greatness of God as creator, sustainer of heaven and earth, as well as the seas. God's sovereignty is all encompassing. The psalmist is also aware of the pagan gods: "the idols of the heathen" (vv.15-18) are lifeless, and the figment of human imagination. According to the writer, they are handcrafted, and without the ability to respond in any way to those who worship them. These are in no way worthy of comparison with the living God who has the capacity to interact with worshipers in a compassionate way (v.14). False gods are not deserving of worship.

Because the first of the Ten Commandments forbids worship of other gods, it makes sense to be devoted to the true God, and avoid any association with idolatry. In King David's time, Zion (in Jerusalem), was the physical location where the presence of the true God dwelt (v.21). It was the focus of worship. The worshipers brought their offerings there for the priests to present to the LORD on their behalf. They received forgiveness for their sins, and were blessed with God's benediction in line with Numbers 6:24 - "The LORD bless you and keep you; the LORD make his face shine upon you and be gracious to you; the LORD turn his face toward you and give you peace." The LORD made a promise to Moses that He will bless His people whenever the priests pronounced this statement. Those who went to the place of worship did so with the anticipation of the blessing.

The New Testament worshipper is an extension of the people of God (1 Peter 2:9). He or she is in the chosen generation that should praise the God who brought them out of darkness into His marvelous light. The same God who loved to dwell in Zion, is present in the service in a church. He also dwells in the spiritual heart of the believer in Christ (1 Corinthians 6:19). This believer goes to church personifying a sacrificial gift, according to the Apostle Paul's recommendation: "Therefore, I urge you, brothers, in view of God's mercy, to offer your bodies as living sacrifices, holy and pleasing to God - this is your spiritual act of worship" (Romans 12:1). Church goers know that there is a benediction after the worship service. This benediction is a big deal for the Lord, just as it was in the Old Testament; it would be beneficial for the believer to anticipate God's blessing as a consequence of praising and adoring Him. The New Testament has at least two benedictions that are frequently used: "May the grace of the Lord Jesus Christ, and the love of God, and the fellowship of the Holy Spirit be with you all" (2 Corinthians 13:14). The second and much longer one is in Hebrews 13:20-21: May the God of peace, who through the blood of the eternal covenant brought back from the dead our Lord Jesus, that great shepherd of the sheep, equip you with everything good for doing his will, and may he work in us what is pleasing to him, through Jesus Christ, to whom be glory for ever and ever. Amen." God's goodness and mercy are said to follow the believer all the time and in all places, both now and forever (Psalm 23:6). It is a good thing to "Praise the LORD."

Suggested Text: Psalm 135.
Suggested Prayer: Psalm 8.

# *Meditation*

*Hear my voice, O God, in my meditation;*
*preserve my life from fear of the enemy.*

*Psalm 64:1, NKJV.*

Some translations like the New International Version (NIV) use complaint instead of meditation. This is so because the Hebrew word siyach has a primary root that means, to ponder, which has a range of meanings including: to converse with oneself or commune, complain, declare, meditate, muse, pray, speak, contemplate (Strong's Exhaustive Concordance). I prefer the word meditate, for it was quite likely in the process of communing with God that King David presented his complaint about wicked men hatching secret plots to slander him. Knowing the solution to his problem, he called on the name of the LORD in a time of difficulty. He was certain that "the righteous shall be glad in the LORD, and trust in Him, and all the upright in heart shall glory" (v.10).

What is meditation? What is its object? What is its objective? How is it done?

Meditation is deep thinking. As the psalmist declared: "Both the inward thought and the heart of man are deep" (v.6b, NKJV). This contemplation can be theocentric or egocentric. The objective of the God-centered variety is to commune with God, and wisely "consider His doing" (v.9). God is held in reverence, trusted, and perceived as available for consultation during prayer. As a result, "The righteous shall be glad in the LORD ... and all the upright in heart shall glory" (v.10).

For the New Testament believer, the meditation process starts by choosing a quiet place and talking to the heavenly Father in secret. According to the recommendation by Jesus in Matthew 6:6, the outcome to be expected is that "your Father, who sees what is done in secret, will reward you" (NIV). The Apostle Paul urged the Colossians to set their affections (or mind's desires) on heavenly things (Colossians 3:1-3).

Essentially, it is a request to apply filters to one's desires as a means of retaining the virtues that make for holiness (vv.4-5). But paradoxically, the individual must interact with the real world, instead of separating from it. The person who meditates does not need to become a monk or a recluse in order to meaningfully commune with God. By being salt and light to the world, the believer's qualities of Christ-likeness get to rub off on those he or she deals with.

The objective of meditation has a few prongs. At heart it is a way of dealing with matters of life and living. The psalmist's desire was this: "preserve my life from fear of the enemy" (64:1b). In this situation the enemy is a tangible and destabilizing force that plots evil by using slander (sharp tongues like swords, arrows, bitter words). Conspirators of this kind will see their own weapons turned against them by the God of the psalmist (vv.7-8). The very tools that the wicked use for evil deeds, can be used by the upright to glorify God. There is another kind of enemy that is not tangible, but spiritual. This is the motivator of evil. This is the guiding principle behind the unrighteous deeds of wickedness (vv.4-5). The lips, mouth, and tongue, are thus influenced negatively to slander and plot evil (vv.3-6). But the LORD is stronger than the forces of wickedness (vv.7-9). The righteous can count on Him to fight their spiritual battles.

Meditation properly done, is God-centered, a means of striving for holiness, and for prayerfully becoming Christ-like. The Father who sees and hears the secret prayer, will reward the person who meditates.

Suggested Text: Psalm 64.

Suggested Prayer: O Lord, I wait on You so that my strength to live for You and for my fellow humans will be renewed day by day.

# Satisfaction

*Better a dry crust with peace*
*and quiet than a house full of feasting, with strife.*

*Proverbs 17:1*

The saying goes, that you should not judge a book by its cover. This can also be applied to family life. Its outward appearance of sufficiency may not be an accurate indication of what goes on inside. The availability of amenities may not guarantee harmony. King Solomon, the writer of the Book of Proverbs, must have known this from experience. He must have seen this in his own family, and that of his father, King David. He undoubtedly saw strife in his royal household.

If the availability of amenities does not make for harmony, what does? Solomon's observations from three texts will shed some light to answer this question. In Proverbs 15:16 and 17, we read: "Better is a little with the fear of the LORD than great wealth with turmoil. Better is a meal of vegetables where there is love than a fattened calf with hatred." Harmony and satisfaction go together. Satisfied people do not start a riot. From the referenced texts it can be argued that "the fear of the LORD" and "love", are antidotes to strife and dissatisfaction. The third antidote is in Proverbs 16:8 - "Better a little with righteousness than much gain with injustice."

Because God has made provision for our satisfaction, we must look at His word to experience it. The Apostle Peter wrote: "His divine power has given us everything we need for life and godliness through the knowledge of him who called us by his own glory and goodness" (2 Peter 1:3). Let us consider what the scriptures say about the fear of the LORD, love, and righteousness.

The fear of the LORD is associated with knowledge, understanding, wisdom, doing God's commandments, and a distaste for sin (Job 28:28; Psalm 111:10; Proverbs 1:7; 15:16). It is not a terror inducing experience. The Bible has many exhortations not to fear. Holding God in awe is not a fearful thing. Living apart from God, is a fearful thing. The fool that says there is no God has a lot to fear because of the lifestyle that is sinful (Psalm 14:1). The Godless are "overwhelmed with dread" (14:5). On the other hand, "God is present in the company of the righteous" (14:5b), and as such, there will be harmony and satisfaction among those who fear or reverence Him.

Love is the second principle for harmony and satisfaction. "Better is a meal of vegetables where there is love than a fattened calf with hatred." God loves completely, because He is love (Psalm 103:8; 1 John 4:8). To reverence God is to be enveloped and indwelled with His love. This love must flow to those who encounter God's people. As such, there will be harmony and satisfaction. The Apostle James calls love the royal law (James 2:8). In his view, those who demonstrate it "are doing right."

Righteousness is right standing with God. In Solomon's view, "Better is a little with righteousness than much gain with injustice." This principle is very important in scripture because God is altogether righteous. He is the LORD our Righteousness (Jeremiah 23:6). Jesus enjoined His audience to seek God's rule and His righteousness as a matter of priority. Consequently all other things (including satisfaction) will be added as well (Matthew 6:33). When people ignore this command, they are very likely to become dissatisfied. Dissatisfied people cannot be harmonious people. They are doing the equivalent of digging cisterns that cannot hold water, instead of tapping the spring of living water made available by the God of Righteousness (Jeremiah 2:13).

Satisfaction and harmony are attainable by putting God first, practicing love, and walking in the way of righteousness.

Suggested Text: Matthew 6:25-34.
Suggested Prayer: Matthew 6:9-13.

# *Gratitude*

*Oh, give thanks to the LORD, for He is good!*
*For His mercy endures forever.*

Psalm 136:1 (NKJV).

Let's say you came across a person on the street and he asks you for money to buy something to eat. You gave him enough to cover a meal and then some. He thanks you and, with a smile on his face, walks away. Some time later you are at work, and while engaged with your tasks, your boss comes and hands you your paycheck. You receive it with thanks and promptly resume your work. You know that your expression of thanks is driven by mere politeness, not to be compared with that of the person you sponsored to get a meal earlier.

Mothers spend time teaching their toddlers how to say please, and thank you. Why? Because these virtues do not come into practice automatically. Even for adults, there is a tendency to regress into ingratitude occasionally. Therefore the psalmist encouraged his people to give thanks to the LORD. Two immediate reasons for this are for the bestowed divine goodness and mercy. The God of Israel was often portrayed as good and merciful. An important aspect of this goodness is mercy. Mercy in the above text is a translation from the Hebrew word, chesed, meaning, steadfast love, or loving kindness. According to the psalmist, this love has no end; it endures forever. Throughout Psalm 136, each verse ends with this refrain. Because mercy is not merited, the receiver will be thankful not just to be polite, but to show heart-felt and overflowing gratitude as well. The exhortation: "Praise the LORD, O my soul; all my inmost being, praise his holy name"(Psalm 103:1), is followed by a verse that ends with: "and forget not all his benefits." The tendency to take granted favors for granted can lead to ingratitude.

Divine love is not conditional. It comes to mankind on account of grace. The New Testament teaches that God loved the world so much that

He sent His beloved Son to atone for its sin (John 1:29; 3:16). God's love is patient, kind, not easily provoked, does not keep a record of wrongs, but rejoices in truth (1 Corinthians 13:4-8, 13). We gain access by faith into divine grace and love through the merits of Jesus Christ, and "rejoice in the hope of the glory of God" (Romans 5:2).

Let us give thanks to the LORD for His mercy endures forever.

Suggested Text: Psalm 136.
Suggested Prayer: Psalm 103:1-6.

# *Prayer and Praise*

*O you who answer prayer, to you all men will come.*
*You answer us with awesome deeds of righteousness,*
*O God our Savior, the hope of all the ends of the earth.*

*Psalm 65:2, 5.*

According to the scriptures, the earth and all its fullness belong to God (Psalm 24:1). This includes you and me. Grace, power, abundance and life, are at the LORD's disposal. He is the hearer of prayers. He has promised to answer even before the petitioner calls (Isaiah 65:24). He is a present help in times of need (Psalm 46:1). Humans are the symbolic sheep of His pasture. So then, why do we need to pray, if like sheep we can have the pasture without asking?

Paradise on earth, Eden, was the geographic location where God met with Adam and Eve, making available to them the fullness of joy (Genesis 3:7-10). This blissful interaction was disrupted by sin. Even in the bleakness of this disruption, there was hope. "The hope of all the ends of the earth and of the farthest seas" (Psalm 65:5) made a promise to reclaim the essence of Eden and crush the evil one (symbolized by the serpent Genesis 3:14, 15). The hope of redemption entails renewed fellowship with God. The psalmist therefore proclaimed: "Blessed is the man you choose and bring near to live in your courts! We are filled with the good things of your house, of your holy temple" (Psalm 65:4). The place where God's honor dwelled was Zion, although He was not limited to that location with His presence. Through prayer and praise believers can enjoy His presence. His ears are open, and His arm is ready to save (Isaiah 59:1). There is forgiveness for the sin that separates us from Him (Psalm 65:3). The atonement for sin, foreshadowed in the animal sacrifices of the Old Testament, is fulfilled in the ultimate sacrifice of Jesus on the Cross of Calvary (John 19:28-30). As a result we can come boldly to the throne of grace to receive mercy and grace in time of need (Hebrew 4:16).

Believers pray as a means of maintaining a conversation with the God of their salvation. This conversation includes adoration, confession, thanksgiving, and supplication or request for assistance either for oneself, or for others. Whether this is done privately, or publicly, as in corporate worship, there is the assurance that such requests will be answered (John 14:13-14).

Suggested Text: John 14:1-14.
Suggested Prayer: Teach me O Lord, to pray correctly.

# *Keeping the Faith*

*So, my dear brothers and sisters, be strong and steady,*
*always enthusiastic about the Lord's work,*
*for you know that nothing you do for the Lord is ever useless.*

1 Corinthians 15:58 (NLT).

This text, if taken in isolation, can serve as the launching pad for a motivational speech. Notice the imperatives: be strong, be steady, be enthusiastic about the Lord's work. Notice also the assurance of the reward for profitable labor: nothing you do is ever useless. Contextually, it is a part of a classical presentation of life and death from the perspective of a believer in Jesus of Nazareth, the first person to come back from the dead, never again to die.

The Sadducees were a sect of Judaism that did not believe in life after death (Matthew 22:23). They fit the category of people with the attitude of: "let us eat and drink; for tomorrow we die" (1 Corinthians 15:32b). Paul warned against this philosophy because it does not acknowledge God (vv.33-34). Those who believe in God know that He is the God of the living (Luke 20:38). Jesus reminded the Sadducees about this when they tried to ridicule the idea of life after death. In our time, one may very well ask: why does this matter? The straightforward answer is that it matters to believe that, what happened to Christ at His resurrection, will also happen to His followers. He is the first fruit of those who die in the faith (1 Corinthians 15:19-26).

The next reason is that this understanding motivates the expectation of a reward for faithful adherence to the teachings of Christ. There is indeed a reward in the final analysis. Therefore this calls for endurance, steadiness and enthusiasm. "If only for this life we have hope in Christ, we are to be pitied more than all men" (15:19). Those who live for the here and now, are described by Paul as pitiful.

The kingdom of God is more than food and drink; and as Paul stated in his epistle to the Romans, "it is righteousness, peace and joy in the Holy Spirit" (Romans 14:17). The kingdom of God, and believers' participation in it, is a good reason to be strong, steady, and enthusiastic about living and working for the Lord now.

Suggested Text: 1 Corinthians 15.

Suggested Prayer: Open my understanding, Heavenly Father, that I may appreciate the vastness of Your provision for this life and that to come.

# *Openness and Closeness*

*Search me O God, and know my heart;*
*test me and know my anxious thoughts.*
*See if there is any offensive way in me,*
*and lead me in the way everlasting.*

*Psalm 139:23-24.*

The essence of a successful relationship is the readiness for openness or transparency between the parties involved. When an individual in a relationship describes the other party as a personal friend, it is probable that they have a close bond. There is however, a closer association than this. It is described as intimate. In it, there are degrees of transparency. "Search me ... and know my heart" is definitely a request for closeness between an individual and deity. This is a prayer for God to search the psalmist's heart. There is no fear in this request. God is love. He can be trusted to honor a close relationship without exploiting it, as the case is between humans.

William Cowper (1731-1800), the author of the hymn "God moves in a mysterious way," also wrote "O for a closer walk with God" (The Revised Church Hymnary). The last two verses of this hymn state:

*The dearest idol I have known,*
*Whate'er that idol be,*
*Help me to tear it from thy throne*
*And worship only Thee.*

*So shall my walk be close with God,*
*Calm and serene my frame;*
*So purer light shall mark the road*
*That leads me to the Lamb.*

"Calm and serene" are the opposite of fear. For Cowper, the thing he knows to be a potential impediment is idolatry. He therefore desires it to be torn away in order to be close to his God. In the New Testament, Jesus beckoned weary and overburdened people to come to Him and learn of Him, in order to find rest for their weary souls (Matthew 10:28). As God the Son, He knew the people's hearts; yet He invited them to come closer and learn of Him. He is Immanuel, God with us (Matthew 1:23). The God who wants to be with His people says: "Come now let us reason together … Though your sins are like scarlet, they shall be as white as snow; though they are red as crimson, they shall be like wool" (Isaiah 1:18). As the subsequent verse notes, willing obedience will result in bountiful benefits. God's complete holiness demands the cleansing for sin, in order to open the way for a meaningful relationship. The psalmist was well aware of this when he prayed: "See if there is any offensive way in me, and lead me in the way everlasting."

The essence of a meaningful relationship is openness. Love is the underlying principle, without a doubt. But it would benefit neither partner where there is no closeness. The psalmist knew this, and so he desired for the all-knowing God to search his heart for any obstacles to the free flow of love. "Love does not delight in evil but rejoices with the truth. It always protects, always trusts, always hopes, always perseveres" (1 Corinthians 13:6,7). "O for a closer walk with God."

Suggested Text: Psalm 139.
Suggested Prayer:
*O for a closer walk with God,*
*A calm and heavenly frame,*
*A light to shine upon the road*
*That leads me to the Lamb!*
William Cowper.

# *Faith and Righteousness*

*But the just shall live by his faith.*

*Habakkuk 2:4 (KJV).*

The prophet Habakkuk was alive before the Babylonians conquered Judah. In his visions, he engaged in dialogues with God. Particularly, he was concerned as to why God would use a wicked kingdom like Babylon to punish His own people (1:12-14). God's response was to the effect that those who are righteous and faithful will live. The proud and the unrighteous will be saddled with the "woes" in chapter two.

King Nebuchadnezzar of Babylon was puffed up with pride on account of his achievements: "Is not this great Babylon, that I have built for the house of the kingdom by the might of my power, and for the honor of my majesty?" The response from God was quick; a voice from heaven declared: "O King Nebuchadnezzar ... the kingdom is departed from thee" (Daniel 4:30-33, KJV). The arrogant king became insane, unfit to rule, and was relegated to living like an animal in the wild.

God opposes the proud, but gives grace to the humble (James 4:6). The Babylonians or Chaldeans, had risen to power by defeating the Assyrians. Their pride and wickedness are attested to by Habakkuk's indictment: "puffed up" and "not upright" (2:4). However, humility and faith are virtues that are compatible with divine grace. Therefore the just (the righteous) shall live by faith. Trusting God by faith was what Abraham did many centuries prior, and he was granted righteousness. God accredited him with righteousness (Genesis 15:6; referenced by Paul centuries later in Romans 4:22).

What is the significance of this? Paul the Apostle of Christ was impressed by this acquired righteous that comes through hearing the Gospel of Christ. He had a good appreciation of Habakkuk's vision (Romans 1:16-17). Justification for the believer is a matter of faith not works. In recent times, a German monk named Martin Luther (1483-

1546), was intrigued by this righteousness apart from works, credited to the believer. His previous understanding, based on church doctrine, was that justification came as a result of divine grace and human good works. "The just shall live by faith" became a rallying cry for the Protestant Reformation. "Therefore being justified by faith, we have peace with God through our Lord Jesus Christ" (Romans 5:1, KJV). Indeed, those who are made righteous shall live by faith through the grace of God. In this state they rejoice in the hope of seeing the glory of God (v.2).

Suggested Text: Habakkuk 2.
Suggested Prayer: My Lord and my God, thank You for the free gift of righteousness.

*Benson Ebinne*

# *Detestable Things*

*There are six things that the LORD hates, seven that are detestable to him.*

*Proverbs 6:16*

Along with a continuing series about human folly, King Solomon lists seven things that the LORD detests. To detest something is to intensely dislike it. In this case, the list includes: haughty eyes, a lying tongue, hands that shed innocent blood, a heart that devises wicked schemes, feet that are quick to rush into evil, a false witness who pours out lies, and a man who stirs up dissention among brothers (Proverbs 6:17-19).

The key word in this text is LORD, which is written with upper-case letters in most English translations from the Hebrew YAHWEH. It is the covenant name of the God of Abraham, Isaac, and Jacob: "the name by which I am to be remembered from generation to generation" (Exodus 3:11-15). Literally, the name means I will be what I will be, or as the translators put it, "I AM WHO I AM" (NIV). The LORD gave His covenant people Israel the Ten Commandments (Exodus 20) as a moral guide in their relationship with Him, as well as with themselves.

The seven sins listed by Solomon can be understood in the light of the Ten Commandments. Because these deadly sins are a breach of the love relationship between God and believers, they must be taken seriously. How should a believer in Christ relate to Proverbs 6:16-19? Reading between the lines, one can approach the text by picturing the opposites of each of these vices i.e., haughty and humble; lying and truthfulness; shedding innocent blood and preserving life; wicked heart and circumcised heart; quick rush into evil and slow to anger; false witness and honest witness; one who stirs up dissention and peacemaker.

The antidote for evil is godliness. From a New Testament perspective, the Apostle Peter spelled out the things that God has provided to enable believers to live a godly life, with the goal of becoming "partakers of the divine nature" (2 Peter 1:1-11). The list includes; faith, virtue, knowledge, temperance, patience, godliness, brotherly kindness, and charity. This is a fruitful life affirming list, compared to the deadly list of Proverbs 6:16-19. As Peter concluded, "if you do these things, you will never fall, and you will receive a rich welcome into the eternal kingdom of our Lord and Savior Jesus Christ" (vv.10-11).

Suggested Text: Proverbs 6:6-35; 2 Peter 1:1-11.
Suggested Prayer: O Lord, lead me in the paths of righteousness.

# Blasphemy

*But whoever blasphemes against the Holy Spirit will never be forgiven; he is guilty of an eternal sin.*

Mark 3:29.

Essentially, blasphemy is an insult directed toward a deity or sacred thing. This insult could be verbal, or implied through a sacrilege (or an irreverent use of a sacred object). Religious people take offense when they hear profanity, or observe disrespect towards their objects of worship. It is good to show respect to people and their religious sensibilities.

The Gospel of Mark records that "the teachers of the law who came down from Jerusalem" (3:22) to Capernaum where Jesus was teaching and healing, and casting out demons, saw what was happening and attributed the exorcisms to Beelzebub. In their conclusions, they maintained that Jesus was using the power of Satan to perform those miracles. They were in effect calling Jesus an agent of Satan. His response was sharp and descriptive (vv. 23-29). He saw their point of view as utterly counterintuitive and ridiculous. If indeed his power came from Satan, it meant that Satan was acting against himself: "And if Satan opposes himself and is divided, he cannot stand; his end has come" (v. 26).

Concerning the mission of Jesus, Mark wrote that the Holy Spirit descended on Jesus soon after His baptism by John the Baptist, "and sent him out into the desert, and he was in the desert forty days, being tempted by Satan" (1:9-13). He was triumphant over the temptations (Matthew 4:1-11), and thereafter began His ministry teaching, healing, and casting out demons. It can be inferred from this that Jesus was working with the power of the Holy Spirit, and not Beelzebub. The miracles of Jesus were tantamount to God's announcement that the kingdom of God was being inaugurated on earth through the Messiah or the anointed one. Spiritual regeneration, transformation, enlightenment, salvation, healing, the raising of the dead, were events being orchestrated by the Holy Spirit, in conjunction with Jesus of Nazareth.

Jesus had earlier on affirmed this when he visited the synagogue in his hometown and was given the honor of reading the selected scripture: "The Spirit of the Lord is on me, because he has anointed me to preach the good news to the poor. He has sent me to proclaim freedom for the prisoners and recovery of sight for the blind, to release the oppressed, to proclaim the year of the Lord's favor" (Isaiah 61:1, referenced in Luke 4:18-19). When He finished reading, He informed the audience that the scripture was about Him. They did not believe that their home boy, the son of Joseph, had messiah pedigree. Jesus knew better.

Therefore, it was an insult to Jesus as well as to the Holy Spirit, for the teachers of the law to attribute His miracles to Satan. Consequently, He made the pronouncement: "I tell you the truth, all the sins and blasphemies of men will be forgiven them. But whoever blasphemes against the Holy Spirit will never be forgiven; he is guilty of an eternal sin" (Mark 3:28-29). There are some believers in Christ who occasionally worry that they might have committed the unpardonable sin. They may be interpreting the above scripture wrongly. This verse is rather a warning to those who in spite of seeing the light, prefer to continue in darkness because their deeds are evil (John 3:16-19).

Suggested Text: Mark 3:20-30.
Suggested Prayer: O Lord, "deliver us from evil: for yours is the kingdom and the power and the glory forever. Amen" (Matthew 6:13).

# Galilee of the Gentiles

*And when He had come out of the boat,
immediately there met Him out of the tombs a man with an unclean spirit.*

Mark 5:2, NKJV.

The fifth chapter of the Gospel of Mark presents the reader with three seemingly impossible and irreversible conditions. The "man with the unclean spirit, who had his dwelling among the tombs" was a menacing danger, and could not be controlled either with chains or fetters. The second condition was the death of a twelve year old daughter of an official of the synagogue. Thirdly, "a certain woman had a flow of blood for twelve years." She had spent all her money for physicians in a vain search for a cure.

The geographic location of these people was a region of ten cities known as the Decapolis, in the northern part of the sea of Galilee. The prophet Isaiah, writing about this region some seven centuries before this time, described it as the Galilee of the Gentiles; and foretold that: "The people who walked in darkness have seen a great light; those who dwelt in the land of the shadow of death, upon them a light has shined" (Isaiah 9:1-2, NKJV). In the lines that followed this introduction, he proclaimed: "For unto us a Child is born, a Son is given; and the government shall be upon His shoulder. And His name will be called Wonderful, Counselor, Mighty God, Everlasting Father, Prince of Peace" (9:6, NKJV).

These lofty attributes spelled out by Isaiah are embodied in Mark's description of the encounter between the demon-possessed man and Jesus of Nazareth. The man called Jesus "Son of the Most High God" (5:6-7). Those of a skeptical mind might question the authenticity of a maniac's pronouncements, especially if he was known to be possessed by a Legion of unclean spirits. (A legion is equivalent to 6,000). Nevertheless, Jesus demonstrated mastery over these demons by exorcising or expelling them. The freed man went away telling dwellers in the Decapolis what

Jesus had done for him. The people were amazed.

Jesus also demonstrated mastery over death by reviving the daughter of Jairus (an official of the synagogue: Mark 5:38-42). This was followed by the healing of the woman with the bleeding condition (5:34). The great light prophesied by Isaiah was indeed shining in the Galilee of the Gentiles. The people were amazed; they could not comprehend it. Could this be the Messiah that was also prophesied by Isaiah? The coming of Jesus signaled deliverance for Israel; particularly deliverance from the bondage of sin (Matthew 1:21). The woman who had been healed was told: "Daughter, your faith has healed you. Go in peace and be freed from your suffering" (Mark 5:34). Here the word for healed is the same as for saved in the Greek, σώζω, pronounced sózó (listed as Strong's number 4982, with a range of meaning including: "deliver, protect, heal, preserve, save" - Strong's Exhaustive Concordance of the Bible).

The demon possessed man and the woman with the illness that plagued her for twelve years, received not only healing but deliverance from the bondage of sin. Jesus came to give His life as a ransom for many (Mark 10:45), and to be the light that enlightens the Gentiles (Luke 2:32). This light that came to the Galilee of the Gentiles is also the light of the world (John 8:12).

Suggested Text: Mark 5.
Suggested Prayer: Open my eyes Lord, that I may see the wonderful works of my Savior.

# Hygiene

*Don't you see that nothing that enters a man
from the outside can make him unclean?
For it doesn't go into his heart but into his stomach,
and then out of his body.*

Mark 7:18, 19.

The gospel writer recorded an incident in which the disciples of Jesus were observed eating their meal without first washing their hands. The Pharisees and some of the teachers of the law asked Jesus why his disciples ignored the practice.

Jesus' response did not impugn the Pharisees for their insistence on ritual cleansing with water. Rather, He criticized the false dichotomy of associating outward cleansing with inward purity. Eating kosher does not make for a kosher heart. According to Jesus, there is a difference between the heart and the stomach. In this dialogue, the heart is a metaphor, not the blood-pumping organ that supplies life-giving oxygen and nutrients to various parts of the body. The spiritual heart is therefore the life-giving pump for the spiritual body. Its integrity and hygiene were being ignored by the outwardly pious Pharisees and teachers of the law. Left unwashed with the water of spiritual hygiene (Psalm 119:9), it becomes the source of "evil thoughts, sexual immorality, theft, murder, adultery, greed, malice, deceit, lewdness, envy, slander, arrogance and folly. All these evils come from the inside and make a man 'unclean'" (7:20-23). It is noteworthy that Jesus prefaced His answer by quoting from Isaiah 29:13, because the religious leaders were paying lip service to God, while promoting their own teachings instead of scripture. As a consequence their hearts were far removed from the Lord whom they pretended to worship.

Why is the heart so important in spirituality? It is where the knowledge of the Lord is birthed and nurtured. "The LORD your God will circumcise your hearts and the hearts of your descendants, so that you may love him with all your heart and with all your soul, and live" (Deuteronomy 30:6). This statement from Moses to the Israelites, about God's desire for a compliant heart, rings true with the prophet Ezekiel's pronouncement about God's intention for the people after the Babylonian exile: "I will give you a new heart and put a new spirit in you; I will remove from you your heart of stone and give you a heart of flesh. And I will put my Spirit in you and move you to follow my decrees and be careful to keep my laws" (Ezekiel 36:26-27). From a New Testament angle, Paul wrote on the same theme of heart transformation: "A man is not a Jew if he is one outwardly, …a man is a Jew if he is one inwardly; and circumcision is circumcision of the heart, by the Spirit, not by the written code"(Romans 2:28-29).

Jesus chided the Pharisees and the teachers of the law for their wrong emphasis on outward appearances. The spiritual hygiene of the heart is more significant for the moral health of the individual, than ritual hand-washings. However, microorganisms (bacteria, parasites, fungi, and viruses) are potentially dangerous, and can be curbed by proper washing of the hands. Such practices are to be encouraged to prevent the spread of infectious diseases. Man looks on the outward appearance, but God looks at the heart (1 Samuel 16:7).

Suggested Text: Mark 7:1-20.
Suggested Prayer: "Create in me a pure heart, O God, and renew a steadfast spirit within me" (Psalm 51:10).

# *Wisdom and Satisfaction*

*Come, eat my food and drink the wine I have mixed.*
*Leave your simple ways and you will live;*
*walk in the way of understanding.*

*Proverbs 9:5-6*

The desire for food and drink is a basic need in the existence of human beings. It is also a metaphor for fulfillment and satisfaction in life. In the animal world, a lot of energy is spent in search for food. Herbivores go about this peacefully, whereas predators do so more forcefully. The goal in all of this activity is satisfaction.

Satisfaction for humans goes beyond having a belly filled with delicious food. Obviously, life is not all about food: "man does not live on bread alone but on every word that comes from the mouth of the LORD" (Deuteronomy 8:3). Because people, like sheep, have a tendency to wander in search of satisfaction, they need wisdom in order to go to the right places to find it. For sheep, there is the shepherd to guide them toward green pastures. For humans, wisdom is the proper guide (Proverbs 4:7-8).

What is wisdom? In general, skill, shrewdness, knowledge, good judgment, and prudence, are aspects of the operation of wisdom in an individual's life. In ethical and religious terms it is the skill required for godly living. Like all skills it improves with good practice. "The fear of the LORD is the beginning of wisdom, and knowledge of the Holy One is understanding" (Proverbs 9:10). Good practice makes perfect. A craftsman does not become a master overnight. His skills are honed through taking and following instructions from the experts. "If you are wise, your wisdom will reward you; if you are a mocker, you alone will suffer" (9:12).

In the reading of Proverbs 9:5-6, King Solomon presents wisdom as a woman of means sending out invitations for a banquet in her mansion.

The invitees are promised a feast complete with meat and wine (vv. 2-4). They are guaranteed satisfaction: "Leave your simple ways and live" (v. 6). By accepting to relocate from their simple means to a place of abundance, they became blessed. Contentment, goodness, mercy (loving kindness), flow in abundance. Similarly, the person who is guided by the wisdom from the LORD, the Holy One, is rewarded with length of days (v. 11). The same cannot be said of the person who responds to the invitation sent out by the woman personified as folly (v. 4). Because her offerings produce death for the invitees (v. 18), this location cannot produce satisfaction.

Suggested Text: Proverbs 9.
Suggested Prayer: Holy Spirit, give me wisdom to cultivate your fruit as found in Galatians 5:22.

# Good Grief

*I grieve for you, Jonathan my brother; you were very dear to me.*

*2 Samuel 1:26.*

David's friendship with Jonathan was unique in the way it progressed. David had been brought to King Saul's court in order to soothe the king who was suffering from bouts of depression and possibly schizophrenia brought on by the evil spirit that was sent to him by God (1 Samuel 16:14-23). Jonathan was the king's son as well as the heir apparent. He took a liking to David. Knowing that his father was bent on harming David, he did his best to keep his friend out of harm's way whenever his father's fits of rage flared up. At a certain stage in their friendship he gave David his princely robe, and made a covenant of friendship with him (1 Samuel 18:3-4; 20:16-17). He had come to terms with the realization that David had been picked to succeed his father as king of Israel.

When David heard the news that his bosom friend was killed in battle he was very grief-stricken. It was as if his blood brother had died. "I grieve for you, Jonathan my brother; you were very dear to me. Your love for me was wonderful, more wonderful than that of women" (2 Samuel 1:26).

The news of a relative's death can be a devastating experience. "There is a friend that sticks closer than a brother" (Proverbs 18:24), as was the case with David and Jonathan. David expressed his grief in the poetic eulogy he wrote about Saul and Jonathan. How should a believer deal with the death of a loved one or friend? Jesus dealt with the death of Lazarus, the brother of his two friends Mary and Martha in a public way. He wept, "Then the Jews said, 'See how he loved him!'"(John 11:35-36). But that was not all. He spoke words of hope to Martha about life after death. He tried to assure her that He was the Resurrection and the Life; and had the prerogative to give this quality to those who put their trust in Him. Martha was understandably confused, as a grieving person, but she had Jesus by her side. Those who believe in Christ can weather the pangs of grief as they hold on to their faith in Him.

Paul the Apostle encouraged the Thessalonians not to grieve like those who have no hope (1 Thessalonians 4:13). He also encouraged the Corinthians to have hope for the resurrection through Christ (1 Corinthians 15:17-22). These assurances have helped grieving Christians to get through the loss of their friends and relatives who died in the faith.

Suggested Text: 1 Corinthians 15.
Suggested Prayer: O Lord, I look on to You, for in You I live and move and have my being.

# *Prayer and Fasting*

*And he said unto them, This kind can come forth by nothing, but by prayer and fasting.*

Mark 9:29 (KJV).

While watching an animated cartoon television show I observed a conversation between a dog and its owner who was holding a cat. As the dialogue continued, the man dropped the cat. The cat landed on its legs after correcting its upside down position in mid-air. The dog was not impressed at all, and showed this by remarking: "anyone can do that!" Thereupon the man picked up the dog, cradling it in his arms just as he did previously with the cat. Then he let it drop. The dog landed on its back.

The disciples of Jesus had observed their master do miraculous acts on many occasions. When they were on their own, they encountered a boy who was frequently tormented by evil spirits that subjected him to bouts of seizures. They tried unsuccessfully to exorcise the evil spirits. The boy's frustrated parents decided to take their boy to Jesus. With a stern command he ordered the evil spirits to leave and never return (v. 25). Later on, in private, the disciples asked Jesus to tell them why they themselves could not accomplish that same feat. He replied: "This kind can come forth by nothing but by prayer and fasting" (v. 29).

Prayer and fasting are disciplines that prepare the believer to face and overcome difficult challenges. A comment from an ex-army combatant speaks volumes for preparedness. He said: "You don't have time to start cleaning your rifle when the enemy strikes." Soldiers habitually clean their weapons to get them ready at a moment's notice. Prayer and fasting are for the Christian what conditioning is for the soldier.

It was the habit of Jesus to withdraw to the hills for prayer. As the God-man, He desired to commune with the Father in order to renew His strength. In this way the challenges of ministering to crowds of needy people were met with biological and spiritual vigor. Those who wait on the Lord shall have renewed strength to fly like eagles, run and walk without exhaustion (Isaiah 40:31). In His comment on prayer, Jesus used the verbs: ask, seek, knock, in the continuous verbal tense. In other words, keep asking and you will receive; keep seeking and you will find; keep knocking and the door will be opened for you (Matthew 7:7-8). He also taught on fasting: that it was to be a private affair between the petitioner and the heavenly Father. He gave this assurance: "and your Father, who sees what is done in secret, will reward you" (7:18).

Sadly, in my observation, prayer is the least emphasized discipline in most churches. The church, which is more or less the house of prayer, allots a proportionately smaller amount of time during worship services to prayer than to other activities like singing and preaching. Prayer in the individual believer's life takes even smaller time slots, compared to other routine activities. Fasting is virtually absent as a Christian discipline.

Like all disciplines, good practice makes perfect. Prayer and fasting condition the believer to be engaged with the Lord's work, and excel in the ministry. Those who delight in the Lord shall have the desires of their hearts met by Him (Psalm 37:4). "Let us then approach the throne of grace with confidence, so that we may receive mercy and find grace to help in our time of need" (Hebrew 4:16).

Suggested Text: Mark 9:1-32.

Suggested Prayer: Almighty Father, I need You every moment of the day to empower me for service. Help me to understand the kind of fasting that is acceptable, as in Isaiah 58.

# Casting Your Bread on the Water

*It is more blessed to give than to receive.*

Acts 20:35

New Testament Scriptures typically described as red letter editions print the quotes attributed to Christ in red. This accounts for red texts especially in the Gospels (Matthew, Mark, Luke and John). Very few words fitting this description can be found in The Acts of the Apostles. "It is more blessed to give than to receive,"- stands out in a field of black letters. It is additionally unique in that this quote cannot be found in the Gospels. It could have been orally transmitted. It cannot however, be classified as apocryphal (not genuine, or authentic).

The Apostle Paul used this quote while addressing a delegation of elders from the church in Ephesus. They had gone to meet him in the city of Miletus where he was making a stop on his return from his third missionary journey. He had previously lived in Ephesus for three years during which "God did extraordinary miracles through Paul, so that even handkerchiefs and aprons that had touched him were taken to the sick, and their illnesses were cured and the evil spirits left them" (Acts 19:11-12). In this farewell address therefore, he emphasized the fact that he had labored with his own hands to care for himself while doing the work of the gospel (Acts 20:34). His motivation was sacrificial love that seeks to help others, especially the weak ones (v.35). He was careful not to exact any pay for his labor of love.

In a way, Paul was imitating the Lord Jesus who stated His mission of sacrificial service to mankind (Mark 10:45). So, what about the quote; "It is more blessed to give than to receive"? Is the absence of evidence, the evidence of absence? In Luke 6:38, there is a hint of this, but not the exact words: "Give, and it will be given to you. A good measure, pressed down, shaken together and running over, will be poured into your lap. For with the measure you use, it will be measured to you." In this context, Jesus was talking about judging, condemning, and forgiving. This is the fabric of human interactions. When it involves love, it brings great returns. It is better to give goodwill.

Suggested Text: Matthew 6:1-4.
Suggested Prayer: Father, help me to be mindful of other people's needs, that I may know that it is in giving that I receive.

# Like Master Like Servant

*Now that I, your Lord and Teacher, have washed your feet, you also should wash one another's feet.*

*John 13:14*

The setting of this statement is the Last Supper that Jesus had with His Disciples on the night in which He was betrayed and subsequently arrested to stand trial. In an apparent role reversal, just before the meal began, He laid aside His garments, tied a towel around His waist, and after pouring water into a basin, started washing the Disciples' feet. After washing each pair of feet, He wiped them dry with the towel. One of the Disciples did not want this treatment. His objection was met with Jesus' insistence to continue, otherwise the objector would be excluded from sharing with the Lord. This Disciple yielded, and had his feet washed.

At the end of this activity, Jesus asked them if they understood what had just taken place. The narrator did not report their response. (Many centuries later, it is not certain that believers in Christ grasp the significance of what happened that night). However, the Disciples were enjoined to follow the example that was demonstrated. The symbolism of Christ's action goes far beyond what was observed that night. What was the Lord's motivation? The opening words in John 13, include: "Having loved his own who were in the world, he now showed them the full extent of his love" (v. 1b). It is possible that Jesus wanted to show what a person who is motivated by love to the fullest extent could do. It is not easy to lay aside pride in order to serve others. This is most likely the example He wanted the Disciples to follow. The one who was essentially God, took upon Himself the form of a servant, and ultimately sacrificed His life to save others (Philippians 2:3-11).

Loving service is possibly the best way to appeal to both friends and difficult people. Paul the Apostle expounded this concept of love as a motivating factor in interpersonal encounters, by pointing to his message in 1 Corinthians 13. He concluded with: "But the greatest of these is love." Next to the Sermon on the Mount, this passage is the most difficult to practice. But it is God who works in the believer to enable its practice (Philippians 2:15).

Suggested Text: Philippians 2.
Suggested Prayer: Lord, give me a servant's attitude, mixed with love and compassion.

# The Original Voice

*The people were amazed at his teaching,
because he taught them as one with authority. ...
He even gives orders to evil spirits and they obey him.*

*Mark 1:22, 27.*

The words authority and author have a common root. An author is the originator of a book or an invention or an idea. Originality is important because that is what makes an author's work special.

Jesus of Nazareth demonstrated originality from an early age. "When he was twelve years old ... Everyone who heard him was amazed at his understanding and his answers" (Luke 2:42, 47). He was "full of grace and truth" (John 1:14). As the author of grace and truth, he commanded authority whenever he spoke. Truth is that which conforms to reality. Those who encountered him were amazed because they were struck by the reality of his actions and words. His teaching was of a higher caliber than that of the teachers of his time, including those before his time. Moses had promised that a prophet will arise and demonstrate more authority than him (Deuteronomy 18:18). John the Baptist who came exercising power like Elijah the great prophet (Matthew 17:11-13) confessed that Jesus was so much more powerful than him, that he will be unworthy to untie his shoes (Luke 3:16).

We observe authority as it is exercised by people who have been invested by a governing power to perform certain duties. When a police constable in the line of duty commands an individual to raise his or her hands straight up, that individual must act in compliance. This is due to the implicit recognition of the governing power that authorized the officer. Jesus of Nazareth had divine authority: "Then Jesus cried out, 'When a man believes in me, he does not believe in me only, but in the one who sent me. I have come into the world as a light, so that no one who believes in me should stay in darkness'" (John 12:44-46).

It is not surprising therefore that Mark noted that "the people were amazed at his teaching" and that evil spirits obeyed His commands. The evil spirits recognized Him as "the Holy One of God!" What people think or know about Jesus is very important. By faith those who believe in Him recognize his power, and thus obey Him because His authority is divine. According to the Apostle Paul, a time is coming when every knee will bow to Him and confess Him as Lord to the glory of the Father (Philippians 2:10-11).

Suggested Text: Mark 1:1-45.
Suggested Prayer: O Lord, we hail the power of Jesus' Name and call him Christ the King.

# Knowing the Will of God.

*When Saul saw the Philistine army, he was afraid;*
*terror filled his heart. He inquired of the LORD,*
*but the LORD did not answer him by dreams or Urim or prophets.*

1 Samuel 28:5-6

Saul was the first king of Israel. He was anointed by Samuel who was the last judge in what was a theocratic system of rule. As king, he had the responsibility of leading his people to fight their enemies. They had to depend on God to fight their battles and win. As a result, the people did not go to war without first seeking divine approval and help. The method of seeking this help was through the effort of the priest who acted as an intercessor to offer prayers on behalf of the king and the people. How did the priest know what God's will was? There were two objects placed in the pouch on the breastplate of the garment (or ephod) that the priest wore before seeking God's will (Exodus 28:29-30). These were the Urim and Thummim, representing glory and perfection respectively. With these he could divine the LORD's will.

King Saul was faced with two dilemmas. He could not use the help of Samuel the priest because he had died. Secondly, there was the huge Philistine army ready to invade his territory. When he attempted to inquire of the LORD, there was no answer either through "dreams or Urim or prophets." Saul did not have a good relationship with the LORD because of his disobedience earlier on when he failed to carry out the divine order to completely eliminate the Amalekites (1 Samuel 28:18). In the face of a looming crisis, he became very afraid and in desperation sought the services of a medium, even though he had banned such practices throughout his kingdom, in conformity with the Mosaic law in Leviticus 19:26, 31; 20:27; Exodus 22:18. Sadly, the king and his son Jonathan were killed during the battle with the Philistines (1 Samuel 31).

"Behold, the LORD's hand is not shortened that it cannot save; neither his ear heavy, that it cannot hear: but your iniquities have separated you from your God; and your sins have hidden His face from you, so that He will not hear" (Isaiah 59:1-2, NKJV). Sin was the impediment in discerning God's will in the time of Saul as it is today. Does God still communicate His will to believers today? Yes. There are people who consult horoscopes in order to know what moves to make. Believers can do better by consulting the word of God, the Bible. Reading, pondering, and obeying God's word, will make the believer stay connected to the wisdom and understanding needed to stay in tune with the will of God. The sure byproduct of this will be success and prosperity. God's instruction to Joshua, the successor to Moses, as he was poised to lead the Israelites into the Promised Land was: "Do not let this book of the Law depart from your mouth; meditate on it day and night, so that you may be careful to do everything written in it. Then you will be prosperous and successful" (Joshua 1:8).

Priests, dreams, Urim and Thummim, were methods of knowing God's will in Saul's time. In the New Testament, and according to Jeremiah 31:31-34, God's law is written on believers' hearts. As such, they will know God's will through the guidance of the Holy Spirit (John 14:15-17). Also, their intercessor is Christ Himself: "but because Jesus lives forever, he has a permanent priesthood. Therefore he is able to save completely those who come to God through him, because he always lives to intercede for them" (Hebrews 7:24-25). He assured His disciples that even though there will be troubles in this life, they should be cheerful because of the ultimate victory He had procured for them (John 16:33).

Suggested Text: 1 Samuel 28:1-25.
Suggested Prayer: "Teach me to do your will, for you are my God; may your good Spirit lead me on a level ground" (Psalm 143:10).

# Conservative Love

*Drink water from your own cistern,
running water from your own well.*

*Proverbs 5:15.*

This is one of several admonitions that King Solomon addressed to his son. These authoritative warnings or exhortations typically opened with phrases like: "my son, pay attention" or, "listen, my son." On this particular occasion the king used poetic metaphors to teach about the seventh commandment (Exodus 20:14). Rather than state the prohibition against adultery, he used word pictures to warn against the bad and the ugly aspects of indiscriminate sexual relations on the one hand, and the goodness of reserved sexual relations in the context of marriage, on the other.

The youth was advised to drink water from his personal source, but not from an outside one. This metaphoric presentation (5:23) was followed by more explicit terms: "May her breasts satisfy you always, may you ever be captivated by her love" (v. 19). God has ordained it this way, and because it is a blessed arrangement it calls for rejoicing: "and may you rejoice in the wife of your youth. A loving doe, a graceful deer" (vv. 18-19). To rejoice is to overflow with joy. The same word is used in the context of worship in the presence of the LORD (Psalm 33:20-21).

Implied in the advice of Proverbs 5:23, is the notion of satisfaction. A satisfied person does not go about looking for more. In this case, captivation, love, affection, and fidelity, are part of a recipe for complete satisfaction. There is blessedness where love, affection, and fidelity exist together under the supervision of the LORD. "For a man's ways are in full view of the LORD, and he examined all his paths" (v. 21). Outside of this prescribed boundary, there exist the bad and the ugly consequences of breaching the seventh commandment. The fruit of adultery may drip with honey, but the end is as "bitter as gall, sharp as a double-edged sword" (vv.3-4). Other regrettable results are listed in verses 9-14: groaning, ruin, and public shame.

In our modern times, there is a confusion of sex and love. I have heard a preacher point out that sex is not the same as love. While this sounds simplistic on the surface, it is scriptural in that love is not restricted, but sex is. There are restrictions on sexual relations in order to prevent its perversion. A whole chapter in the book of Leviticus is devoted to these restrictions. Leviticus 18 opens with a warning that God's people should refrain from indiscriminate sexual relations; and ends with a command for them to keep from defiling themselves. The New Testament upholds these principles with a summary statement: "It is God's will that you should be sanctified: that you should avoid sexual immorality; that each of you should learn to control his own body in a way that is holy and honorable, not in passionate lust like the heathen, who do not know God" (1 Thessalonians 4:3-5).

Suggested Text: Proverbs 5.
Suggested Prayer: Father, help us to realize that we are individually the temple of the Holy Spirit.

Benson Ebinne

# *Vigilance*

*Therefore keep watch,
because you do not know the day or the hour.*

Matthew 25:13

This short verse is characterized by a warning and a command. To fully understand their impact one must consider the context. Matthew 25:1-13 is known as: "The Parable of the Ten Virgins." The narrator is Jesus Himself as the third party in this account of the preparation for an Israelite wedding ceremony. The activities leading to its consummation are comparable to the activities leading to the consummation of the Kingdom of Heaven. The bridegroom arrives long after he is expected (v. 5). In this particular story, he arrived around midnight after the bridesmaids (or virgins) had fallen asleep. The announcement woke up the bridesmaids who quickly went into action to get their oil lamps ready. Five of them found out that their lamps were out of oil. Their request for oil was turned down by the other five. The only alternative was to go out and buy some oil. They returned from their trip to find out that the bridegroom had arrived and that the door to the ceremony was shut. The chilling response from the bridegroom on the other side was that he truly did not know them (v. 12). Those who came prepared are called T*he Wise Virgins,* while the unprepared ones are called The Foolish Virgins. The subtle moral to the story: be careful, and do not let yourself suffer loss.

The significance of this warning is to be prepared for the time when the Son of Man comes. Otherwise, people will miss out or not be let into the kingdom. Obviously Jesus was referring to His Second Coming to set up the Kingdom of Heaven (or the Kingdom of God) on earth. The Lord's Prayer has a petition for this Kingdom: "Thy kingdom come, Thy will be done on earth, as it is in heaven" (Matthew 6:10, KJV). Preparation as well as preparedness for this event requires vigilance. In any game, the opposing team invariably earns a point at the particular juncture when the other team was not vigilant enough to detect a costly maneuver by the scorer. At the end of the game, the winner is welcomed with cheers, while the losers are met with tears. The Foolish Virgins made a tactical error by not checking their lamps ahead of time.

Believers in Christ must "keep watch" because they "do not know the day or the hour" of His coming. They can take some hints from the advice that was given to Joshua, the successor to Moses, as he was poised to enter and take the Promised Land. The LORD told him: "Do not let this Book of the Law depart from your mouth; meditate on it day and night, so that you may be careful to do everything written in it. Then you will be prosperous and successful" (Joshua 1:8). The word of God, from the Books of Genesis to Revelations, is for reading, meditation, obedience, and practice. Victory belongs to those who pay attention to its principles, and through the inspiration of the Holy Spirit, stay prepared for the coming of the Son of Man.

Suggested Text: Matthew 25:1-13.
Suggested Prayer: Lord, keep my lamp burning until You return.

# *Spiritual Stirring*

*So the Lord stirred up the spirit of Zerubbabel son of Shealtiel, governor of Judah, and the spirit of Joshua son of Jehozadak, the high priest, and the spirit of the whole remnant of the people. They came and began to work on the house of the LORD Almighty, their God.*

Haggai 1:14

I have a niece who does a lot of stirring while cooking. In sharp contrast to her, I keep this action to a minimum. When she meets me cooking, she cannot restrain her urge to stir what I am working on. She is probably more in tune with nature than me, because in nature, where things have a tendency to settle under the influence of gravity, it becomes necessary to disturb the process more or less to suit the operator's plans. Therefore, the cook mixes up the ingredients in the pan or pot to keep them from settling and scorching. Besides, the stirring helps to blend flavors that could otherwise stay apart.

How does this apply to intangible things like people's spirits? We know from experience that the law of inertia applies to physical and intangible things alike. Psychologically, people form habits that prove difficult to break. A given state of affairs will continue until it is otherwise interrupted by an opposing force. This applies to spiritual matters as well. In the Bible, there are accounts of human beings interacting with the God of Abraham, Isaac and Jacob, on a spiritual level. Although God is a spirit, He is relational, rational, emotional, and volitional. These attributes are communicable to humans. When God's people tend to become spiritually lethargic or lukewarm, or cold, God stirs them up to reverse the inertia of complacency.

The Book of Haggai details the complacency that had gripped the returned exiles from Babylon. Back in Jerusalem, they had begun work to restore the Temple that Solomon had built (that the Babylonians under King Nebuchadnezzar had destroyed some seventy years prior - 2 Chronicles 36:15-20). Two years into the repair project, a combination of circumstances like the lack of resources and the opposition from their opponents, stalled the progress. Their zeal was diminished and subsequently extinguished. For eighteen years they settled into taking care of their personal affairs to the exclusion of rebuilding the Temple. They however did not fare well because bad weather, poor agricultural harvests, financial losses, lack of satisfaction, combined to make their lives miserable. The inertia of diminishing returns overtook them.

Therefore the LORD began the stirring process from the top (Haggai 1:14). People from every level of society became reenergized spiritually, and they resumed the rebuilding project they had abandoned. They were admonished to reorder their priorities: "Give careful thought to your ways" (vv. 5, 7). They were assured of continued divine accompaniment: "I am with you" (v.13). For the Christian, the antidote to spiritual complacency is to order first things first, in the service of the Lord. "Seek first the kingdom of God and his righteousness and all these things will be added" (Matthew 6:33). God is at work using His people to do His good purposes (Philippians 2:13).

Suggested Text: Haggai 1:1-14.
Suggested Prayer: Lord, stir my spirit and keep me shining that I may have the zeal to serve.

# *Praying to Be Answered*

*If anyone turns a deaf ear to the law, even his prayers are detestable.*

*Proverbs 28:9*

There is a definite link between listening or hearing, and obedience. A stubborn youth is often described with such phrases as: *he does not listen; in through one ear, and out through the other.* Such an individual will find it difficult to have his requests satisfactorily granted by his parents. I remember an occasion during my secondary school years, when I had a pressing need for money to buy something for my school work. Because I did not want my father to know about it, I approached my mother for help. She responded: "ask your father. After all, you always do what he says!" With such bolstered confidence I presented the need to my father, and was granted.

"If anyone turns a deaf ear to the law, even his prayers are detestable." This statement from King Solomon had a basis in the scriptures. Law in this statement is the *Torah*, according to the Hebrew text, and it refers to the *Five Books of Moses* or the Pentateuch. The teachings, instructions and regulations attributed to the God of Israel, can be found in these books. They are centered on love. "Hear, O Israel: The LORD our God, the LORD is one. Love the LORD your God with all your heart and with all your soul and with all your strength" (Deuteronomy 6:4-5). This command further states how to show this love: by observing "these commandments that I give you today" (v.6), as recorded in Deuteronomy 5:1-32, and declared to the hearing of those present. Being attentive as well as observant were indicative of obedience and love for the law giver. By the same token, turning a deaf ear to them was tantamount to holding back the love due the law giver, thereby short-circuiting the love current. The prayers of such a disobedient person become detestable.

The ability to obey the LORD is a gift of grace. The believer functions in a family relationship where the LORD is the Father. This relationship has been made possible through the obedience of the Son of God (John 1:11-13). Jesus described the text in Deuteronomy 6:10, as the greatest commandment, to the extent that (together with Leviticus 19:18) the Law and the Prophets hang on it (Matthew 22:37-40). When believers living in a redeemed relationship love the Lord, they can pray and also expect answers. "He who did not spare his own Son, but gave him up for us all - how will he not also, along with him, graciously give us all things?"- Romans 8:32.

Suggested Text: Romans 8.
Suggested Prayer: "Open my eyes that I may see wonderful things in your law" (Psalm 119:18).

*Benson Ebinne*

# *So Near and So Far*

*Those who devise wicked schemes are near, but they are far from your law.*
*Yet you are near O LORD, and all your commands are true.*

*Psalm 119:150-151.*

The cry for help is the central theme of this psalm (119:145-152). It is a desperate call for help where the enemy was advancing and gaining ground in a menacing way. "I call with all my heart; answer me, O LORD, and I will obey your decrees" (v.145). Like a youngster running from bullies in the neighborhood, his home is closer at the same rate that his pursuers are closing in. And then he gets there at the moment that his father is opening the door. Those bullies know they do not belong there. They run the risk of incurring the wrath of the boy's father.

This situation reminds me of a hymn, "*God is always near me.*"

God is always near me,
Hearing what I say,
Knowing all my thoughts and deeds,
All my work and play.

God is always near me;
In the darkest night
He can see me just the same
As by mid-day light.

God is always near me,
Though so young and small;
Not a look or word or thought,
But God knows it all.

The Revised Church Hymnary (Oxford University Press), lists this hymn by Philipp Bliss (1838-76) under "For Little Children." However, it is appropriate for adults as well. The realization of God's presence watching over us is comforting, but could be taken for granted when life is running smoothly. During such times, prayers may become a ritual routine engaged in with little or no fervency. Emergencies jolt believers from such smooth sailing. The storm stirs up the waves and our boats are rocked and tossed. Consequently we call for help, not with fanciful words, but with screams! The psalmist called with all his heart to be delivered from "Those who devise wicked schemes" (v. 150). They may be near God, but not in their devotion. They are opposite God's will, in that they are far from God's law (law in the sense of the Torah or the Books of Moses, where God's covenant is recorded). They do not pay attention to the covenant terms or stipulations to honor and obey God in order to enjoy the covenant blessings. As such they are not in good terms with the LORD. Deuteronomy 28 lists some of these terms under blessings and curses for obedience or disobedience respectively.

The psalmist's promise to obey the LORD's decrees means that he is in good terms with his God. As such he can count on His loving kindness and justice (vv. 149-150). The enemy's threat for today's believer may not necessarily be physical. It could be spiritual. As Paul notes in Romans 7:21-24, there is a tug-of-war between good and evil taking place in him. His rescuer is Jesus Christ. Victory over sin and temptation, or any other hardship in life, can be achieved by calling on the Lord's name. Whoever calls on the name of the Lord shall be saved. Like the psalmist, any believer can say: "I call to you; save me and I will keep your statutes" (119:146).

Suggested Text: Psalm 119:145-152.
Suggested Prayer: Lord, I affirm with the prophet Isaiah that no weapon formed against me shall prosper (Isaiah 54:17).

# *Heart Conditioning*

*Keep your heart with all diligence, for out of it spring the issues of life.*

*Proverbs 4:23, NKJV.*

The heart, as presented in scripture, is the seat of emotion as well as intelligence. In this chapter however, it is depicted in three verses (4, 21, and 23) only as the repository of things heard by way of instruction. Wisdom, understanding, doctrine, law, and knowledge, come into it through the windows of the eyes and ears. The hearer is admonished to get wisdom and understanding. This is because; "Wisdom is the principal thing; therefore get wisdom. And in all your getting, get understanding" (vv. 5, 7, NKJV).

Exposure to relevant information is helpful in building and maintaining a point of view. In the era of television, cell phones, smart phones, radios, and the internet, the likelihood of being distracted is tremendous. Some people like to keep their television sets or their radios on all the time. Some others can sustain telephone conversations for hours. While all these electronic devices are very important in contemporary living, their uncontrolled use can adversely affect those moments of reflection that are necessary for the nourishment of the proverbial heart. The inner self can use a break from the modern frenetic pace of life to recharge the *batteries* within. Reflection, meditation, quiet time, time out, are synonyms for the creation of moments for rumination necessary for analyzing and retaining useful information to fortify the mind psychologically, spiritually, and intellectually.

There was a time when I realized the adverse effects of these distractions personally. Take television newscasts for instance. Whenever possible, I made sure to watch them. This was in addition to the hourly newsbreaks on radio. Then it dawned on me that most of what I was watching or listening to concerned accidents, natural disasters, crime, violence, and conflicts of varying degrees of severity. As a result I turned off my car radio, home radio, television set; and went on a self-imposed electronic media fast for more than six weeks. My guiding principle was; "keep your heart with all diligence, for out of it spring the issues of life" (v. 23). The benefit for me was the breaking of a habit that had kept me going to the news media for information that was not helping my intellect or psyche.

It is possible to pollute the heart with the wrong load of information. The fourth chapter of Proverbs presents both dos and don'ts regarding the maintenance of the heart. The biological heart must be kept healthy and fit through good nutrition and exercise. By the same token, the proverbial *heart* must be kept healthy and fit through spiritual and moral discipline, because out of it spring the issues of life.

Suggested Text: Proverbs 4.

Suggested Prayer: "Create in me a pure heart, O God, and renew a steadfast spirit within me" (Psalm 51:10).

# Clear Conscience

*Paul looked at the Sanhedrin and said, "My brothers,
I have fulfilled my duty to God in all good conscience to this day.*

*Acts 23:1.*

What exactly did the Apostle Paul mean when he made the claim about a good conscience with regard to his duty to God? What is conscience? "It is a sense of right and wrong, with an urge to do right" (Webster's New World Dictionary). On another occasion he made a similar remark: "So I strive always to keep my conscience clear before God and man" (Acts 24:16). He was certain about this word and what it meant to him (see also 1 Corinthians 4:4; 2 Corinthians 1:12; and 2 Timothy 1:3). Does this mean that he had a good conscience all through his life, or did he acquire this virtue after he became a follower of Christ? I would argue for the latter situation considering that he was a persecutor of the earliest Christians (Acts 9).

The opposite of a good conscience is guilt. Deliverance from guilt is a spiritual condition that conforms to conversion. "When Christ came as high priest ... he went through the greater and more perfect tabernacle that is not man-made ... He did not enter by means of the blood of goats and calves; ... but he entered the Most Holy Place once for all by his own blood, having obtained eternal redemption" (Hebrews 9:11-12). This unique sacrifice was efficacious to "cleanse our consciences from acts that lead to death so that we may serve the living God" (v. 14), because Christ "died as a ransom" to set sinners free (v. 15).

Paul spoke of possessing a good conscience because of his grasp of what was accomplished by Christ on the Cross for all mankind. In his court appearance before the Sanhedrin, he was reprimanded by the high priest Ananias, who consequently ordered him to be slapped on the mouth (Acts 23:2) for making such a bold claim. Most likely, this high priest had not yet received the grace of God for salvation and deliverance, to cleanse his conscience, as described in Hebrews 9:14. All those that the Lord has called to serve Him, "must keep hold of the deep truths of the faith with a clear conscience" (1 Timothy 3:9).

Suggested Text: Hebrews 9:1-15.
Suggested Prayer: "Search me, O God, and know my heart; test me and know my anxious thoughts. See if there is any offensive way in me, and lead me in the way everlasting" (Psalm 139:23-24).

# True and Reasonable

*I am not insane, most excellent Festus ...*
*What I am saying is true and reasonable.*

Acts 26:25

The Apostle Paul never wasted any opportunity to tell his audience about his conversion testimony because his encounter with the risen Christ was a turning point in his life as a Jew and a Pharisee. This happened as he was traveling to Damascus, with authority from the Jewish religious leaders in Jerusalem to arrest Jews who had converted to the Way (as the belief system of the followers of Christ was known at that time). In his zeal, he was in the habit of going "from one synagogue to another to have them punished, and ... tried to force them to blaspheme" (26:11). His experience of that event, which put a stop to this nefarious activity, was the story he was narrating to Governor Festus seated in court with his invited guest, King Agrippa, some years later. At this time, he himself was arrested and brought to court for disturbing the peace, and as a member of the Way.

"I saw a light from heaven, brighter than the sun, blazing around me and my companions" (26:13), Paul explained as he recounted his conversion experience. He continued to recount what followed, as from this radiance a voice called him by name and demanded to know why he was persecuting the owner of this voice. Then the awe struck Paul asked the voice to identify itself. "I am Jesus, whom you are persecuting" (26:15). Then he was given instructions including the fact that he will become a servant and a witness of what he had just experienced. He was also instructed about where he should go to immediately (26:16-18).

As the governor and his invited guest from Jerusalem listened, Paul linked his impression of Christ to the Jewish scriptures. "I am saying nothing beyond what the prophets and Moses said would happen - that the Christ would suffer and, as the first to rise from the dead, would proclaim light to his own people and to the Gentiles" (26:22-23). The governor, a Gentile, could not bear all this religious talk from Paul. The account of the resurrection of Jesus was too much to take. Therefore he remarked: "You are out of your mind, Paul ... Your great learning is driving you insane" (26:24). Paul responded: "I am not insane, most excellent Festus. What I am saying is true and reasonable" (26:25).

Is the resurrection of Jesus true and reasonable? Is it reasonable to believe such a fantastic story? As Paul would state later in his letter to the Corinthians: "the message of the cross is foolishness to those who are perishing, but to us who are being saved it is the power of God" (1 Corinthians 1:18, NKJV). Without the new birth, as recorded in John 3:1-23, no one can see (v. 3), let alone enter (v. 5), the kingdom of God, because "that which is born of the Spirit is spirit" (v.6, NKJV). Spiritual things are spiritually discerned (1 Corinthians 2:14). Paul was convinced about his conversion. He was also convinced that Jesus Christ was alive. No one could gainsay his testimony: not even Governor Festus. For Paul, these matters are true and reasonable.

Suggested Text: Acts 26.

Suggested Prayer: Open my eye O Lord so that I can see wonderful things from the Bible.

# *The Whole Truth*

*But Samuel said, "How can I go? Saul will hear about it and kill me. The LORD said, "Take a heifer with you and say, 'I came to sacrifice to the LORD.'"*

1 Samuel 16:2.

After the rejection of Saul as king of Israel, it was necessary to appoint a replacement. Samuel, the man of God, was appointed to undertake the anointing of the next king. This person would come from one of the sons of Jesse in Bethlehem. The problem for Samuel was that he will attract the attention of the current king's men as he traveled to Bethlehem from Ramah where he lived. Such a venture would put his life in danger. This dilemma was presented to the LORD, who therefore advised Samuel thus: "Take a heifer with you and say, 'I have come to sacrifice to the LORD.'" With this plan, he could then carry out the secret mission of anointing the new king without arousing the anger of King Saul.

Did the LORD ask Samuel to act deceitfully? The dictionary definition of deceit includes lying and dishonest action. Before attempting an analysis of this text, it would help to consider two other texts: "He who is the glory of Israel does not lie or change his mind, for he is not a man that he should lie" (1 Samuel 15:29; see also Numbers 23:19). The God of righteousness will not lie because that is not His nature. Did His instruction to Samuel amount to a lie? The obvious answer should be no, considering that one of the Ten Commandments forbids the giving of false testimony (Exodus 20:16). Samuel indeed used the heifer to perform a sacrifice. What he did after that ceremony was not Saul's business. It would have been counter productive to let Saul in on it.

Believers are committed to the truth because God is the advocate of truth. There is no unrighteousness in Him. Jesus, God with us, is the way, the truth and the life (John 14:6). He came that we may have life abundantly (John 10:10). If someone with murderous intent comes asking me if I know where his intended victim was hiding, I would refuse to provide him with the information to accomplish his goal. He is not entitled to know the truth in this case. A lie is the corruption of truth for selfish ends.

Suggested Text: 1 Samuel 16:1-13.
Suggested Prayer: Heavenly Father, give me wisdom to be as crafty as a serpent and harmless as a dove.

*Benson Ebinne*

# The Master and His Servant

*Hear, O LORD, and answer me, for I am poor and needy.*
*Guard my life, for I am devoted to you.*
*You are my God; save your servant who trusts in you.*

*Psalm 86:1-2.*

The relationship between a servant and his master is a dynamic one. It is also delicate and symbiotic. A good master insures the welfare of his servant because he is dependable and productive. In certain parts of Africa where cattle are still raised the old fashioned way, a cow herder takes charge of some twenty cattle and leads them from one grazing field to another. Sometimes he would do this on a planned route covering many miles, to a city where he sells them to a businessman. This middleman then sells the animals to butchers who transport them to the nearest slaughterhouse. Usually, the butcher employs young men who must transport the animals by walking them or forcing them to run. The means of controlling them is through two ropes: one around the neck and the other around a hind leg. The journey can be slow at times because of resistance on the part of the unwilling cow. The resistance is countered with prodding and pulling. There is no cooperation; no give and take like it used to happen with the cow herder on those long trips.

The psalmist recognized a give and take dynamic in his relationship with his God. He was aware of his poor and needy state. He was dependent on a very basic level. He knew about devotion and trust. His life was more or less in the hands of his master. What then was the master's responsibility? The master cares through hearing and answering, as well as guarding (keeping) his servant. LORD (the translation from the Hebrew word Yahweh) is the covenant name of the God of Abraham, Isaac, and Jacob (Exodus 3:16). In this covenant relationship, He binds Himself to take care of His people, who in turn bind themselves to honor their obligations of obedience and devotion (Exodus 24:3-4), in a relationship of trust. Therefore, David was aware of this covenant relationship when he prayed: "save your servant who trusts in you" (Psalm 86:2).

Believers in Christ are in a covenant relationship with God through Jesus, the Son of God. "This is my blood of the new covenant, which is poured out for many for the forgiveness of sins" (Matthew 26:28). This is a reference to the covenant ratification in Exodus 24. Similarly, those who are in Christ can count on the Father to care for them through thick and thin. Jesus had promised that whatsoever believers ask in His name will be granted.

When believers take His yoke of service, and find rest for their souls, they become servants of the Lord (Matthew 11:28-30). In this state they can count on their Master to care for them every step of the way.

Suggested Text: Psalm 86:1-17.
Suggested Prayer: Lord, help Your servant to be faithful and obedient.

# *The New Covenant*

*And he took bread, gave thanks and broke it, and gave it to them, saying,
"This is my body given for you; do this in remembrance of me."
In the same way, after the supper he took the cup, saying,
"This cup is the new covenant in my blood, which is poured out for you."*

*Luke 22:19-20.*

These words are familiar to Christians who have taken part in a Communion Service (or The Lord's Supper, or the Eucharist). Jesus was the one speaking and the symbols of bread and wine were part of the Passover meal that was being celebrated that night. The Feast of Passover (also known as The Feast of Unleavened Bread) was instituted by God as a remembrance of the time when the Israelites in Egypt were spared the death of their first born males as He executed judgment on Pharaoh, king of Egypt, for his stubborn refusal to set the enslaved Israelites free (Exodus 12). The Israelites were commanded to use the blood of an unblemished lamb in each household, to mark the door frames (sides and tops). "The blood will be a sign for you on the houses where you are; and when I see the blood, I will pass over you. No destructive plague will touch you when I strike Egypt" (12:13). The slaughtered lamb was to be roasted and eaten hastily, with unleavened bread, and bitter herbs. When the time came on that eventful night, the death of the Egyptian first born males, and animals, broke Pharaoh's resistance, causing him to declare the Israelites free.

The Passover tradition was observed in the time that Jesus was on earth, and still is even till modern times. When He personalized the elements of bread and wine as His body and blood respectively, it was something new to his audience during that meal. Reading between the lines, some of them possibly realized that He was going to be the Passover Lamb (being full of grace and truth, - John 1:14 - He was unblemished). But He also mentioned "the new covenant in my blood, which is poured out for you" (Luke 22:20). Again, reading between the lines, some in His audience might have remembered the old covenant at Mount Sinai, where the blood of sacrificed animals on that occasion was sprinkled on the people, to confirm the covenant (Exodus 24:8). There the people bound themselves in a covenant with God, and promised to do everything the LORD said (24:3).

Centuries later, the prophet Jeremiah foretold a time when a new covenant will be enacted. Unlike the covenant at Sinai when the law was written on tablets of stone, the new one will be written on the hearts of individuals (Jeremiah 31:31-34). Whereas Moses sprinkled the blood of sacrificed animals on the altar and on the people for the atonement of their sins, the new order's atonement for sin will be mediated by the blood of the Lamb of God. The Apostle Peter who was present at the Last Supper, affirmed this, years later, in his letter or epistle: "live your lives as strangers here in reverent fear. For you know that … you were redeemed from the empty way of life … with the precious blood of Christ, a lamb without blemish or defect. He was chosen before the creation of the world, but was revealed in these last times for your sake" (1 Peter 1:17-20).

"The blood of goats and bulls and the ashes of a heifer sprinkled on those who are ceremonially unclean sanctify them so that they are outwardly clean. How much more, then, will the blood of Christ, who through the eternal Spirit offered himself to God, cleanse our consciences from acts that lead to death, so that we may serve the living God!" (Hebrews 9:13-14). The blood of the new covenant was poured out for the forgiveness of sins (Matthew 26:28). On account of this the Lord has promised not to remember the sins of believers anymore (Jeremiah 31:34). May these thoughts refresh our minds every time we take the Lord's Supper, and always!

Suggested Text: Matthew 26:17-30.
Suggested Prayer: Lord Jesus, thank You for the sacrifice made for the forgiveness of my sins.

# *Honoring God*

> *Honor the LORD with all your wealth,*
> *with the firstfruits of all your crops;*
> *then your barns will be filled to overflowing,*
> *and your vats will brim over with new wine.*
>
> *Proverbs 3:9-10*

Material things are tangible: we can see them, feel them, use them, cherish them, or even despise them. Some of them make life comfortable. They are a means to an end. Often, we think that material things are all there is as far as possessions are concerned, because people define wealth by these visible signs. But there is more to life than these. The word "wealth" in the NIV is translated as "substance" in the KJV. The dictionary definition presents various meanings for substance including: essential nature, ultimate reality that underlies all outward manifestations, material possessions, etc.

What does it mean to honor the LORD with all your substance or wealth? Each person is endowed or gifted with time, talent and treasure. Some people know how to use one or more of these gifts. Others have developed ways to optimize their use. There is the joke about the new comer to New York trying to find his way to Carnegie Hall (a concert venue). Stopping to ask for directions, he said to a local: "How do I get to Carnegie Hall?" He replied: "Practice, practice, practice." There are those who are very practiced in their use of time, talent, and treasure. Their wealth can be assessed in the distinct ways in which they manifest their assets. Some use their assets for self indulgence, while others use them to benefit others. Humanitarians and philanthropists fall into the latter category. People of faith do this in the name of God, and thus are honoring the Lord with their time treasure and talent. Their efforts will not go unrewarded. The Israelites who were commanded to do this with the firstfruits of their crops, were promised barns "that will be filled to overflowing" as well as vats that "will brim over with new wine" (Proverbs 3:9-10). In an agricultural economy, it is easier to determine what firstfruits are, than in a non-agricultural one. The initial early maturing crops would fit this category.

How does this apply to a New Testament believer in a mixed economy? An all encompassing definition of firstfruits in the Merriam-Webster's Collegiate Dictionary states: "the earliest products or results of an endeavor." The believer in Christ gives not out of coercion, but freely, because the Lord loves a cheerful giver (2 Corinthians 9:6-7). He or she realizes the returns, and appropriately honors the Lord. Honoring the Lord is based on the recognition that the earth and all its fullness belong to Him (Psalm 24:1). The possessor of time, talent and treasure, first and foremost belongs to the Lord, whose mercy and grace are freely given to all. Paul the Apostle advises believers: "see that you also excel in this grace of giving" (2 Corinthians 8:7). Two verses earlier, he commended the believers in Macedonia because "they gave themselves first to the Lord … in keeping with God's will." Therefore the Christian's devotion and discretion are integral parts of determining what wealth and firstfruits to give to the Lord who, though He lacks nothing, desires the wholehearted love of believers (Deuteronomy 6:5, Hosea 6:6).

Giving and generosity are related, although people might think of them only in terms of material goods. Time, talent and treasure, are within reach of everybody. Some people have one item more than the others. Each person is gifted in such a way that with proper cultivation of them he or she can become rich, and serve as a source of generosity to other people. "Do not withhold good from those who deserve it, when it is in your power to act" (Proverbs 3:27). This advice is appropriate not only for helping others with money or goods, but also with time and talent.

Suggested Text: Proverbs 3:1-35.
Suggested Prayer: Lord, help me to be a generous and cheerful giver.

Benson Ebinne

# *Dust in the Wind?*

*Teach us to number our days aright,
that we may gain a heart of wisdom.*

Psalm 90:12.

This is one of six petitions in this psalm dealing with the brevity of life, in the context of the infinite God and His anger against sin. The other five are: *relent, satisfy, make us glad, reveal, and favor.* What is the importance of teaching the people to number their days? It is so "that we may gain a heart of wisdom." Wisdom in the scriptural sense is the skill necessary to live a godly life (Job 28:28; Proverbs 1:7). The petition in Psalm 90:12 comes at the end of an account acknowledging three important facts. The God who created the universe is everlasting. This God has accommodated His people. There is a direct link between death and sin (Genesis 2:15; Ezekiel 18:20).

It is this link between sin and death that people seemingly fail to realize or acknowledge. According to Moses, death is the divine sentence on man for the sin of disobedience. "We are consumed by your anger and terrified by your indignation" (v. 7). Genesis 3, especially verse 19, asserts: "dust you are and to dust you will return." Adam and Eve did not suffer sudden death following their disobedience because of God's mercy.

There are knowledgeable people who explain away death as a biological disintegration. Biblical wisdom beckons all to come to grips with the consequences of sin. Moses, the writer of this psalm, also wrote the book of Genesis. His prayer in this psalm was a request to God to teach His people about the consequences of sin so that they may know why life has been limited to approximately seventy or eighty years (v. 10).

Even though the first half of this psalm is grim, the second half presents hope. God may be angry and indignant (v. 7), but He is also relenting, compassionate, and loving (vv. 13-14). He is ready to "establish the work of our hands" (v. 17), as believers incline toward His will.

The New Testament sheds more light on the hope the believer should have. The Apostle Paul taught that justification was God's gift of grace which acquits the sinner, rendering him or her righteous through the atoning work of Jesus Christ: "so that, just as sin reigned in death, so also grace might reign through righteousness to bring eternal life through Jesus Christ our Lord" (Romans 5:21). Believers do not become dust in the wind after their earthly existence. The proposal in Psalm 90:17 corresponds with the often heard benediction: May the grace of our Lord Jesus Christ, the love of God, and the fellowship of the Holy Spirit be with you now and forever, (derived from 2 Corinthians 13:14). Grace, love and fellowship are the hallmarks of God's abiding presence. We therefore rejoice in the hope of God's glory knowing that our union with the Lord Jesus shields us from divine wrath while granting us everlasting life. "For if, when we were God's enemies, we were reconciled to him through the death of his Son, how much more, having been reconciled, shall we be saved through his life! Not only so, but we also rejoice in God through our Lord Jesus Christ, through whom we have now received reconciliation" (Romans 5:10-11).

Suggested Text: Psalms 90:1-17.
Suggested Prayer: Lord, I pray for grace to walk circumspectly, and live wisely.

# *Prayer Principles*

*Watch and pray so that you will not fall into temptation.
The spirit is willing but the body is weak.*

*Matthew 26:41*

*Watch,* is a word that comes with a range of meanings. It involves observation in order to pay special attention and preempt any undesirable outcome. You watch a pot of oatmeal on a stove to keep its contents from boiling over. You watch your steps while walking on a slippery surface so as to keep from slipping and falling. There is however a variety of watching that is less demanding: you watch a game for entertainment purposes. The players have to watch their game seriously, but the spectators do not need to.

The injunction to watch and pray, that Jesus uttered to his disciples in the Garden of Gethsemane, was significant because it required them to pay special attention in order to avoid undesirable consequences. The occasion was the night in which Jesus was betrayed. He had taken the disciples to a secluded area for the purpose of prayer. The engagement was a spiritual exercise that required focus. But the disciples were drowsy and lapsed into deep sleep, rendering themselves unequal to the task of watching, let alone praying. Prayer as a spiritual exercise entails the observation of certain principles that Jesus portrayed on the fateful night in which He was betrayed. A close look at Matthew 26:36-46 will reveal these principles:

1. Choosing a quiet place: v. 36. Gethsemane was a garden where Jesus had a habit of withdrawing to with His disciples (John 18:2).

2. Involving close friends: vv. 37-38. Peter and the two sons of Zebedee (James and John), were the inner circle of Jesus' disciples. A shared burden becomes lighter; so Jesus let them know his burden: "My soul is overwhelmed with sorrow to the point of death. Stay here and keep

watch with me" (v. 38).

3. Going on, alone for a one on one with the Father, seeking His will: v. 39.

4. Fighting fatigue: v. 40. This serious stumbling block to prayer has to be taken seriously. Busy people lack prayer discipline because of tiredness. Jesus was focused, but His disciples were drowsy.

5. Being vigilant to preempt temptation: v. 41. Jesus was vigilant to pray in order to preempt the temptation to bypass drinking the cup of death (v. 39). The disciples' lack of vigilance and prayer left them susceptible to deserting Jesus at the crisis moment.

6. Being steadfast by going for the second round of praying: v. 42. At this juncture, Jesus dropped the petition to bypass the cup. He yielded: "… may your will be done." This petition, for the Father's will to be done, is reminiscent of The Lord's Prayer in Matthew 6:9-13.

7. Persevering for a breakthrough: v. 44. Jesus "prayed the third time, saying the same thing." Prayer in essence is the attempt to align one's intentions and desires with God's will. Proverbs 3:5-6, instructs the believer to trust the Lord completely, and acknowledge Him to lead him or her in a straight path.

With these seven principles, Jesus has left us an example of how to pray and gain victory concerning the burdens and obstacles believers face in their daily walk with God. The word of God assures believers that everyone who asks will receive (Matthew 7:8). The verb is in the continuous tense, meaning that everyone who keeps on asking will receive. It is God's will that we should bring our burdens to Him. "Cast your cares on the LORD and he will sustain you; he will never let the righteous fall" (Psalm 55:22).

Suggested Text: Matthew 26:36-46.
Suggested Prayer: O Lord, help me to trust and obey You, as I seek Your will for my life.

# *Shalom*

*I will say of the LORD,*
*"He is my refuge and my fortress, my God, in whom I trust."*

Psalm 91:2.

This psalm is full of guarantees that are at first sight unbelievable, in that they are amazingly fantastic. In the previous chapter, God is portrayed as indignant about sin (90:7-12), but in this one He is described with such words as: refuge, fortress, trustworthy, and faithful. His protection guarantees that no harm will befall those who trust and obey Him.

Having lived in rural areas where hawks and other predatory birds can be a menace to chickens, I know how vulnerable the chicks become when the predator is engaged to kill and eat. The alert mother hen however, would sound an alarm on such occasions, summoning all her brood to quickly scurry under her wings for safety. Consequently the hawk has no choice but to back off.

The psalmist uses superlative terms like: the Most High, the LORD, my God, to describe his protector, under whose wings he can take cover from all the dangers that threaten him (v. 4). What are these life-threatening dangers? They are: the snare or trap of the fowler, the pestilence or fatal epidemic disease, the terror by night, the arrows or plague by day, the lion, the poisonous snakes, the dragons, or any other harmful things. The guarantee of protection comes in the form of assurances like: "No harm will befall you, no disaster will come near your tent" (v. 10), because he loves the LORD (v. 14). The protection comes with an added empowerment to trample the lion and the serpent (v. 13). God's promise of protection comes to those who place their trust in Him and also love Him (vv. 2, 14).

Love and trust work well together in a relationship, but nothing should be taken for granted. The same principle applies in a spiritual relationship with God. For example, the Snake Handling Churches in Appalachia and some other places, presume on divine protection (using scriptures from Mark 16:17-18, Luke 10:19, Acts 28:1-6) in their deliberate use of poisonous snakes, as well as drinking poisonous solutions, during worship services; on the grounds that these would not harm them. For an outsider looking at them, this is more or less an exercise in tempting God. Psalm 91:11-12, was used by Satan during the temptation of Jesus, to which He replied: "It is also written: 'Do not put the Lord your God to the test'" (Matthew 4:5-8). The guarantee of God's protection and security does not permit the believer to undertake risky activities. The Lord is faithful and loving. His mercy is everlasting, and His truth endures to all generations.

In the New Testament, the Son of God assured His Disciples: "I have told you these things, so that in me you may have peace. In this world you will have trouble. But take heart! I have overcome the world" (John 16:33). This promise is for present day disciples of Christ as well. We are more than conquerors through Christ (Romans 8:37). We can say of Him: "He is my refuge and my fortress, my God, in whom I trust."

Suggested Text: Psalm 91:1-16.
Suggested Prayer: Lord, I surrender all to You for complete protection and welfare.

# Lord Have Mercy

*Behold, as the eyes of the servants look to the hand of their masters,*
*as the eyes of a maid to the hand of her mistress,*
*so our eyes look to the LORD our God, until He has mercy on us.*

*Psalm 123:2 (NKJV).*

For those who do not have a domestic system where servants play a prominent role, it may be difficult to visualize the picture that is being painted by the psalmist. Servants in such a system are tuned in with eyes and ears to the demands of their masters or their wives. Attentiveness is the key to the efficient functioning by the servant. Eye contact may not be appropriate either while receiving instructions or while making petitions. But the eyes must watch all important gestures.

In this psalm, the servant has petitions. The master is the LORD, God of Abraham, Isaac and Jacob. Harking back to Psalm 121, the description of the LORD as the protector and helper who watches His people with constant attention, is a reminder to the petitioner that help is always available. Therefore, in any situation of need, and especially when the enemy is mounting unbearable oppression, divine intervention can be counted on for relief.

It has been observed that those churches that have growth in membership do so because they create an environment of worship where people come expecting God to help them. They are encouraged to have spiritual eyes that look up to the hand of God. In worship, there is singing and there is also praising. And by faith there is the expectation for answers to prayers. Coming boldly to the throne of grace to find mercy in time of need (Hebrew 4:6), is not the same as begging. A child comes to the parent to request favors that are available just for the asking.

There is a difference between a beggar and a servant. A beggar has no relationship with the person being petitioned. However, a servant has a relationship with the master who is being petitioned. There is a symbiotic relationship which is very important. The beggar has no obligation to the giver. But a servant is obligated to obey and respect the master. In this situation, the master's hands and their signals are well known and understood. The hymn writer, Philip Doddridge (1702-51) wrote:

*Ye servants of the Lord,*
*Each in his office wait,*
*Observant of His heavenly word,*
*And watchful at His gate.*

*Watch: 'tis your Lord's command,*
*And while we speak He's near;*
*Mark the first signal of His hand,*
*And ready all appear.*

*O happy servant he,*
*In such a posture found!*
*He shall his Lord with rapture see,*
*And be with honour crowned.*

*(The Revised Church Hymnary,*
*Oxford University Press).*

We, like the psalmist, do encounter "much contempt … much ridicule from the proud … much contempt from the arrogant" (123:4), but we can be sure that the one who is able to keep us from falling, is powerful enough to vindicate us and show us divine favor (Jude 25).

Suggested Text: Psalm 123:1-4.

Suggested Prayer: "Because of the LORD's great love we are not consumed, for his compassions never fail" (Lamentations 3:22). Thank you Father for Your unfailing love.

Benson Ebinne

# *The Hope of God's Glory*

*Not only so, but we also rejoice in our sufferings,
because we know that suffering produces perseverance; perseverance
character; and character hope. And hope does not disappoint us,
because God has poured out his love into our hearts by the Holy Spirit,
whom he has given us.*

Romans 5:3-5.

As I was driving to an appointment one morning, I listened to a program on the radio featuring a comedian. Her routine was based on her experiences, particularly on the occasion when her boyfriend dumped her. Not only that, she had just lost her job, and coincidentally found out she was pregnant.

I arrived where I was going and turned off the radio without hearing the rest of her story. After my appointment I got into the car and continued to listen to the same station, except that another program was playing. This time the topic was about the usefulness of failure. Adversity, as they opined, can be a springboard to success.

Again, I could not stay in my car long enough to hear the conclusion of a discussion about the goodness of failure. This time I arrived at my next stop to attend a church service. The sermon topic was about the significance of suffering in a believer's life. The sermon text was taken from the letter to the Romans 5:1-5. As the preacher spoke I began to connect the dots as I recalled the predicament of the young woman who lost her boyfriend and her job at the same time that she discovered her pregnancy. I placed this alongside the notion of the advantages of adversity. The problem of suffering is food for thought for philosophers, theologians, comedians, and lay people alike. People handle life's difficulties in a variety of ways. Some seek help from friends and relatives, while others become withdrawn, and like a disturbed turtle, retract into a shell of denial and depression. Yet, others look to alcohol for temporary relief;

but others fight back and refuse to accept defeat.

The writer of Romans 5:1-5 knew and experienced adversity, suffering and pain on several levels and occasions (2 Corinthians 11:25). From Paul the Apostle, we learn that the proper foundation for dealing with suffering is faith in Jesus Christ (the man of sorrows who was acquainted with grief - Isaiah 53:3). On a spiritual level, Jesus supplies the grace for believers to exercise hope when faced with adversity. Paradoxically, "suffering produces perseverance; perseverance, character; and character, hope. And hope does not disappoint us, because God has poured out his love into our hearts by the Holy Spirit, whom he has given us" (Romans 5:3-5).

Suggested Text: Romans 5:1-11.

Suggested Prayer: Loving Heavenly Father, in all our afflictions You are also afflicted. Give us grace and faith to weather the storms of suffering and adversity.

# Fair Play

*During the reign of David, there was a famine in three successive years; so David sought the face of the LORD.*

*2 Samuel 21:1*

*Justice and fair play*: how often do we hear this phrase? Kids say it differently: *"that's not fair."* The covenant God of Israel had cried foul on account of what King Saul did to the Gibeonites by decimating them (v. 5). Even though they were not Israelites, they were given part of the land that was apportioned to the Benjamites after the conquest of Canaan. The reason for this was their covenant with Joshua to protect them. Joshua and the elders of Israel were not aware of the deception of the Gibeonites (Joshua 9:15, 18-26). It was too late when the elders found out that the Gibeonites did not want to be wiped out with the Canaanites. Four centuries later, Saul as king, decided to punish their descendants. The LORD was displeased with Saul for violating a treaty that was entered into with the LORD as witness. He showed this by imposing a famine that lasted for three years.

King David succeeded Saul. And it was during his reign that the famine took place. So he went into a prayer session described as seeking the face of the LORD (v. 1). It was then that David was informed by revelation from the LORD about the breach of the covenant by Saul. As the epitome of justice and fair play, the LORD is known for keeping promises; and especially those that are made in His name. One of the virtues of a godly person is that "he keeps his oath even when it hurts" (Psalm 15:4). How does God speak to His people? Through: circumstances, signs and wonders, dreams and visions, human conscience, other people's views and suggestions, and any other means by which God has kept His people informed (the scriptures, for instance). David was certain that the LORD had given him the answer. He was also required to right the wrong that King Saul had caused.

David consulted the Gibeonite representatives to find out what they wanted done in order to satisfy their anger and pain for Saul's injustice. Their response is recorded in 2 Samuel 21:1-2. David granted their wish and thus satisfied the LORD as well. "After that, God answered prayer on behalf of the land" (21:14b).

This story has lessons for us today, as it had for the people about three thousand years ago: The God of righteousness is a promise keeper who wants people to keep their promises, especially those made under oath. Wrongs must be righted whenever possible. Those who seek the LORD in prayer will find answers. God has power to withhold rain, and to give it. "Surely the arm of the LORD is not too short to save, nor his ear too dull to hear. But your iniquities have separated you from your God; your sins have hidden his face from you so that he will not hear" (Isaiah 59:1-2).

Suggested Text: 2 Samuel 21:1-14.

Suggested Prayer: Lead me Lord, in the paths of righteousness, for Your Name's sake. Help me to keep promises I make to others.

# *Covetousness*

*Achan replied, "It is true! I have sinned against the LORD,
the God of Israel. This is what I have done:
When I saw in the plunder a beautiful robe from Babylonia,
two hundred shekels of silver and a wedge of gold weighing fifty shekels,
I coveted them and took them.*

*Joshua 7:20-21.*

It is a well known fact that dubious acts done in secret eventually become exposed and publicized (Luke 12:3). Achan's act of squirreling some plundered goods during the fall of Jericho was expertly done. He alone knew where the goods were hidden. Humanly speaking, desiring to have worldly goods to make life comfortable is not necessarily bad or evil. In Achan's case, the means of acquisition was problematic from the start. He was fishing in troubled waters, and he knew it. He could not enjoy his loot because the goods were extracted from a place that was under God's curse and judgment. All of Jericho was under cherem, a Hebrew word described by Strong's Exhaustive Concordance as: "a doomed object, cursed thing appointed to utter destruction; a thing devoted to God." It was the LORD's prerogative to dispose of things that are banned. By possessing objects covered by cherem, Achan became a part of the curse, and it was only a matter of time before what he had done caused the loss of lives for thirty-six men (v. 5), as well as distress for Joshua, the people, and ultimately the death of Achan and his family (vv. 24-26).

The process of yielding to temptation is typical, as described by Achan himself: "When I saw in the plunder a beautiful robe … two hundred shekels of silver … I coveted them and took them" (vv. 20-21). In the New Testament, the apostle James noted a similar scenario: "but each one is tempted when, by his own evil desire, he is dragged away and enticed. Then after desire has conceived, it gives birth to sin; and sin, when it is full grown gives birth to death" (James 1:14-15). Achan reaped the result of his selfish action: "He who is caught with the devoted things shall be destroyed by fire, along with all that belongs to him. He has violated the covenant of the LORD and has done a disgraceful thing in Israel" (7:15).

The believer in Christ who gets entangled in sin may not meet such a drastic end as Achan. "If we claim to be without sin, we deceive ourselves and the truth is not in us. If we confess our sins, he is faithful and just and will forgive us our sins and purify us from all unrighteousness" (1 John 1:8-9).

Suggested Text: Joshua 7:1-26.
Suggested Prayer: "A broken and contrite heart, O God, you will not despise" (Psalm 51:17).

# *Fountain of Life*

*The mouth of the righteous is a fountain of life.*

*Proverb 10:11.*

When the modern urban dweller hears the word fountain, she is very likely picturing a mechanically generated jet of water rising up and then falling into a pool. There is however another kind of fountain: a natural and unforced stream of water coming out of the ground. It may form a pool or it may continue flowing to form a river. From either of these two pictures, the flow produces a bigger quantity of water than at its beginning. If the source is polluted, the pool will be polluted as well. If it is clean at the source, the pool will be clean also.

King Solomon's analogy in Proverbs 10:11 indicates that a righteous person's mouth will produce a life-giving flow of words. The instruments of speech (lips, mouth, tongue - vv. 13, 11, and 19, respectively), must be used wisely in order to perform their God-given purpose. The following quotes support this purpose:

> Wisdom is found on the lips of the discerning (v. 13).
> Whoever spreads slander is a fool (v. 18b).
> The tongue of the righteous is choice silver (v. 20).
> The lips of the righteous nourish many (v. 21).
> He who holds his tongue is wise (v. 19).
> The mouth of the righteous brings forth wisdom (v. 31).
> The lips of the righteous know what is fitting (v. 32).

A sweet smile inevitably shows on the face of a person being showered with compliments. The opposite effect is demonstrable when a person receives uncomplimentary remarks. "A word aptly spoken is like apples of gold in settings of silver" (Proverbs 25:11). As a result the believer has an obligation to use the power of speech in ways that please the Lord, and edify the hearer. In the New Testament Jesus warned His audience that every individual will give an account of every careless word spoken (Matthew 12:36). The Apostle Paul advised: "Do not let any unwholesome talk come out of your mouths, but only what is helpful for building others up according to their needs, that it may benefit those who listen" (Ephesians 4:29). The verse immediately following this command, states: "And do not grieve the Holy Spirit of God, with whom you were sealed for the day of redemption." Simply put, unwholesome talk (corrupt communication, in the KJV) grieves the Lord.

The natural person has difficulty exercising tongue discipline. A Christ-centered person can possess that discipline through the power of the Holy Spirit. The exhortation in Ephesians 4:29, to avoid corrupt or unwholesome talk but rather to engage in speech that helps to build others up, is followed in the next verse with a command: "And do not grieve the Holy Spirit of God, with whom you were sealed for the day of redemption." From this one can conclude that the Holy Spirit's desire is for Christians to use polished speech. Therefore a prayer for divine help daily should come in this form: "May the words of my mouth and the meditation of my heart be pleasing in your sight, O LORD, my Rock and my Redeemer" (Psalm 19:14).

Suggested Text: Proverbs 10:1-14.
Suggested Prayer: Father, I need Your power to discipline my speech, so that I may build others up.

# *Dominion and Glory*

*But we see Jesus, who was made a little lower than the angels, for the suffering of death crowned with glory and honor, that He, by the grace of God, might taste death for everyone.*

Hebrews 2:9, NKJV.

This verse begins with the interjection but, indicating a contrast from the preceding sentence that also begins with but. In that sentence the writer was advancing the argument that contradicted the reality of a quote from Psalm 8:4-6, in which the psalmist was extolling the majesty of the God who made the heavens and the earth, including man whom He crowned with glory and honor. Furthermore, according to the psalmist, all things were placed under the dominion of man. In reality, however, man in general does not appear to be in control over all the created things.

The writer of Hebrews therefore observed a prophetic note in Psalm 8:4-6, which he interpreted with a messianic link. Viewing the incarnation of Jesus as a starting point he portrayed The Son of God as "the radiance of God's glory and the exact representation of his being, sustaining all things by his powerful word" (Hebrews 1:3). This is the one who though God in essence, he humbled himself and took the form of a human being, for the purpose of atoning for the sins of man. He came and tasted death for everyone (2:9). After accomplishing this feat, he was exalted to sit "at the right hand of the Majesty in heaven. So he became as much superior to the angels as the name he has inherited is superior to theirs" (1:4). This is the one who has dominion over all things. He also procured a relationship between His Father, and the redeemed. "For both he who sanctifies and those who are being sanctified are all of one, for which reason He is not ashamed to call them brethren" (2:11, NKJV).

Through His atoning sacrifice, Jesus destroyed the power of the devil (2:14), and thus retains dominion of all things. All believers in Him are

His joint heirs, and also have dominion over the creation, just as the psalmist declared (Psalm 8:4-6).

Suggested Text: Hebrews 2:1-11; Psalm 8:1-9.
Suggested Prayer: "O LORD, our Lord, how majestic is your name in all the earth."

# *A Note of Thanks*

Thank you one and all, for reading these meditations. I hope the scripture passages with a range of topics have stimulated a desire for reading more of the Bible. I pray these meditations inspire you to acquire knowledge, deepen your knowledge of the God who inspired them, and think of ways to apply this knowledge to enhance your love for Him and our fellow humans.

As a token of my appreciation, please let me share with you a few poems that I have written over the years.

# Selected Poems by Benson Ebinne

## Love... With Care

Speaking of love,
The words of an adage advise:
"Handle it like an egg."

Behind the walls of that shell,
Brittle in its integrity,
Symmetrical in its beauty,
Elliptical in its dignity,
Lie the issues of life
Yet to be explored
Waiting to be adored.

I've watched a race
Whose performers compete
Each with a fresh egg
Balanced on a spoon
And ready to run a hundred yards,
Ensuring that the egg stays intact
At the finish line.

I look at you and my eyes wonder
How I can balance you on a spoon
And run from the South Pole
Straight to the North Pole
Overcoming all the obstacles:
The mountains, the rivers,
The beauties of creation,

*Benson Ebinne*

The rains, the storms,
The snow and the heat …
With you still balanced
In the spoon of my arms.

You came to me
Wrapped in a package
With the inscription:
"Handle with care."

# Habitat

I live where the rubber meets the road,
Right there in the crevices of concrete,
Where friction and rarefied air
Makes it hard for my lungs to breathe.

I live where the rubber meets the road,
Right there, where penury, mixed with greed,
Causes one brother to live by taking
Another person's life, just to satisfy a need.

In the habitat where the rubber meets the road,
There exists the ecology of degradation.
Everybody appears the same when the wicked strike;
For, vice is cloned with a dark face.

Life where the rubber meets the road,
Has taught me many lessons indeed.
Puddles collect water and become ever deeper,
And as the furious tire splashes water -

On apathetic bystanders,
A brief reaction to the rude splash
Vanishes and is forgotten in the rinse cycle.
But I am left where the rubber meets the road.

Occasionally the street sweeper rumbles by,
Lashing his revolving brushes, to cleanse me.
I am left tickled by these temporary measures:
Band-Aid applications, to stanch the tears,

I live where the rubber meets the road.
Don't ask me why I do. I just live there.

*Benson Ebinne*

# Let's Talk Again

Love that does not talk dies.
I seek to forestall such demise.
For who will be there to eulogize
The sad, severed bond?

The bustle of daily life,
With its attendant chaos and strife,
Has helped to sharpen the knife
That could have cut this bond.

The bond that has stayed these many years
Is the balm that calmed my fears,
Often, has stemmed the flow of tears
From my care worn eyes.

I seek to talk to you, more
Than I've done in days of yore.
Ere this stalemate eats me like a sore,
Tell me you love me.

Then I'll sing you a new song
From a heart that's vibrant and strong.
Our love is young.
And will last forever.

# Ruminations

Memories from days gone by
Leave ripples on my mind.
Waves (restless then, mellow now)
Stroke my thoughts and leave behind
Sea shells, debris, and polished stones.
Every now and then I pick up these stones
Desiring to hold and keep them.
But then, I return them
As if afraid to disturb
The ecological equilibrium
Of the pulsating shoreline.

*Benson Ebinne*

# Habits of Evasion

We are all wounded soldiers
In the battle for life.
But we camouflage our wounds
With habits of evasion.

No one sees the bandages.
The wounds are sterilized
As we walk straight-faced
While the cancer of pretence
Eats the fibers of our being,
Leaving behind shreds:
Worn out sentiments,
Dying resolutions,
Ulcers that must ooze
In the long run.

# Tangibles and Intangibles

## *Part I*

### *Tangibles*

Love comes everyday.
It comes just to stay.
We bask in its glow
And drink from its flow.
The huge waves beat
But cannot unseat
The Rock of Gibraltar.
Love cannot falter.
This genuine attribute
Deserves our salute.

## *Part II*

### *Intangibles*

Love comes and goes.
Ballet dancers pirouette
And skip on their toes.
What will they think of next?
The fever ebbs and flows.
We must read life In its clear context.
Love comes and goes.

*Benson Ebinne*

# Mon Ami

You know that I have tried.
You wiped the tears I cried.
You knew my desire
And thus kindled my fire.
You saw I was afraid
You reached out and stayed
The forces of detraction,
And gave me satisfaction.

When you saw my doubt
You restored my clout.
When I needed confidence
You came to my defense.
What more can I ask?
There's just no task
You've let me tackle alone.
You're the best friend
I've ever known.

# Notes

# *Acknowledgments*

This book was made possible through the grace and mercy of the Lord, to whom I am thankful.

I am grateful to my family for the support and cooperation I received in the process. In particular, I want to thank Runyi, one of my offspring, for her tireless editing and suggestions.

For comments, please email me: ***omonohguy@gmail.com***

www.ingramcontent.com/pod-product-compliance
Lightning Source LLC
Chambersburg PA
CBHW071459070526
44578CB00001B/395